WHEN PROPHETS SPEAK OF JUDGMENT

HABAKKUK, ZEPHANIAH, HAGGAI

BY DAVID M. LEVY

The Friends of Israel Gospel Ministry, Inc.
P. O. Box 908, Bellmawr, NJ 08099

WHEN PROPHETS SPEAK OF JUDGMENT
HABAKKUK, ZEPHANIAH, HAGGAI

Copyright © 1998 by The Friends of Israel Gospel Ministry, Inc.
Bellmawr, New Jersey 08099

Levy, David M.

Printed in the United States of America
Library of Congress Catalog Card Number: 98-072175
ISBN 0-915540-35-5

The Friends of Israel Gospel Ministry, Inc.
P. O. Box 908, Bellmawr, New Jersey 08099

Cover by Left Coast Design, Portland, OR

WHEN PROPHETS SPEAK OF JUDGMENT

HABAKKUK, ZEPHANIAH, HAGGAI

BY DAVID M. LEVY

TABLE OF CONTENTS

DEDICATION

This book is lovingly dedicated to my dear wife Beverly, who sacrificially gives of her time and talent to my ministry, and whose spiritual insight is invaluable. Habakkuk is one of her favorite books. The prophet's message continues to be a source of personal strength and encouragement to her. She has found the words, "Yet I will rejoice in the LORD, I will joy in the God of my salvation" (Hab. 3:18), to be especially meaningful.

PREFACE

The tenth century B.C. was the golden age of Israel. Solomon ruled over the nation and exceeded all the kings of the earth in riches and wisdom. The queen of Sheba doubted these reports about Solomon and traveled to Jerusalem to see for herself. Upon touring Jerusalem and hearing the wisdom of Solomon, she reported, "behold, the half was not told me: thy wisdom and prosperity exceedeth the fame which I heard" (1 Ki. 10:7). But Solomon eventually did evil in the sight of the Lord and did not follow Him fully, as did David his father. He married many foreign women who, in his old age, turned his heart to other gods. He allowed altars to be built in Jerusalem for Ashtoreth, Milcom, Chemosh, and Molech, which was an abomination to the Lord (1 Ki. 11).

After Solomon's death, Israel suffered decay, decline, and division, largely due to Solomon's pride, arrogance, unbridled passions, idolatry, and oppressive taxation of the people. The seeds of rebellion sown during Solomon's reign produced a revolt against Rehoboam, his son and successor. Rehoboam was unwilling to heed the advice of Israel's elders, who requested that concessions be made to ease the people's burden of compulsory service and excessive taxation. Rehoboam's reluctance to ease Israel's burden precipitated revolution and division within the kingdom, led by Jeroboam, the son of Nebat (2 Chr. 10). Jeroboam became the ruler of the northern kingdom, called Israel, composed of ten tribes with Samaria as its capital. Rehoboam remained ruler of Judah, the two southern tribes, including Levi, with Jerusalem as its capital.

Jeroboam, although not a religious man, knew that he must set up an alternate system of worship in Israel. This would eliminate the need for the people to make worship pilgrimages to Jerusalem and would assure undivided loyalty to his rule. He set up golden calves to be worshiped in Bethel and Dan. Men were chosen to function as priests, but not from the Levitical priesthood, in direct disobedience to God's law (1 Ki. 12:26-33). Soon Baal worship replaced true worship in Israel, as idolatry flooded the land. Jeroboam's ungodly strategy laid the foundation for Israel's demise.

God reached out to Israel in love by raising up prophets to warn the nation of its apostasy. But every attempt to woo the people back to uncompromising faithfulness failed. The prophets' messages of repentance and renewal went unheeded. In 722 B.C., Israel was totally destroyed by the Assyrians. The prominent people within the ten tribes were taken to Assyria as slaves, and the area was repopulated with Gentiles. These Gentiles married the poor remnant of Israelites left in the land, and the group became known as Samaritans. For centuries, this area remained blighted by pagan worship.

God, however, extended grace to Judah. He allowed the nation time to turn from idolatrous worship and escape the destruction that had befallen the ten tribes of Israel. In the reigns of Hezekiah and Josiah, great reforms were accomplished. Judah put away idol worship, kept God's law, and enjoyed a measure of peace and prosperity. But after Josiah's untimely death, his son Jehoiakim plunged the nation into wickedness. Judah returned to idolatry, gross iniquity, and social injustice. Once again, God raised up prophets such as Habakkuk and Zephaniah to warn Judah that failure to repent would result in God's judgment on the nation. But the nation refused to heed the pleading messages of the prophets to repent and reform.

Under Jehoiakim's reign, God raised up the Babylonian Empire, which forced Judah to become a vassal state. In time, Jehoiachin, son of Jehoiakim, and other nobles of Judah, were exiled to Babylon by King Nebuchadnezzar. Nebuchadnezzar installed a puppet king, Zedekiah, in Judah. The people pressured Zedekiah to revolt against Babylon, which produced swift retaliation by the Babylonians. In 586 B.C., they besieged and burned Jerusalem and Solomon's Temple, leaving only a remnant of people in Jerusalem under the rule of Gedaliah, the governor.

God's purpose was accomplished in the punishment of sinful Judah by 70 years of captivity in Babylon. This captivity ended when Cyrus the Persian issued an edict in 536 B.C. permitting all Jews in Babylon to return to Jerusalem. Restoration was accomplished under the leadership of Zerubbabel, Ezra, and Nehemiah. Moral and religious life was reestablished, and the Temple was completely rebuilt by 516 B.C.

The experiences of Judah wave a warning sign for today. Nations or individuals who engage in wickedness—whether it be idolatry, gross immorality, or social injustice—will eventually pay the penalty for their iniquity. They will suffer God's wrath as Judah did. History has shown that God, who is sovereign judge in the universe, does not change. He will recompense nations in every generation for the evil they commit.

The prophets of Judah prepared the nation for what was coming. Messengers like Habakkuk and Zephaniah provided a blueprint for survival that, if followed, would have stayed God's hand of judgment. Yet Judah did not heed God's warning through His prophets.

Often people in our day, like those in Judah, smugly smile at the thought of judgment coming to their country. They write off those who bring such messages as out-of-touch doomsayers living in a bygone era. These people are living only for the moment. Swamped with the pressures of family and job, they give only a passing thought to their personal destiny, let alone that of their country. The frantic pace of life keeps many people from standing back to contemplate the big picture of life. Those who do not heed the warning signs are in danger of having no sense of history. They forget that judgment has befallen all the great nations of the past that turned away from God and followed evil.

But history need not be repeated; judgment need not come. God places messengers in every nation, in every age, to awaken the conscience of the people to return to God. The Bible is replete with examples of God's using a remnant of people to perpetuate the survival of a country. It takes only one person—like an Ezra, a Nehemiah, or a Jonah—to turn a nation back to God. May each of us be stirred by the messages of Habakkuk, Zephaniah, and Haggai to be that one person to turn this nation back to God.

PART I
HABAKKUK

INTRODUCTION

Habakkuk's name means *embrace*. A number of rabbinical legends developed around his name. Some scholars believe that Habakkuk was the son of the Shunammite whom Elisha embraced when he raised him from the dead. This is because of the phrase, "thou shalt embrace a son" (2 Ki. 4:16). Others say he was the man referred to by Isaiah (Isa. 21:6; cp. Hab. 2:1) who was set to watch the fall of Babylon. Still others view him as the man sent by an angel to feed Daniel pottage and bread when he was in the lions' den (Apocryphal book, *Bel and the Dragon*). Legends are just that—legends. They developed around Habakkuk because nothing is known of his background, lineage, hometown, or occupation. Some believe he was a Levite because he wrote, "To the chief singer on my stringed instruments" (3:19). We do know that he was a prophet of Judah (1:1) and a contemporary of Jeremiah, Ezekiel, Daniel, and Zephaniah. Thus, he probably lived in Jerusalem.

The date of Habakkuk's prophecy has been disputed through the centuries. An approximate date is determined by aligning the events described by the prophet with the history of Judah. Conservative scholars believe the book was written during the reign of Jehoiakim (609-597 B.C.) for the following reasons.

1. The Chaldeans had not invaded Judah as yet (1:6ff; 2 Ki. 24).

2. There is no record of the 70-year Babylonian captivity that took place in 586 B.C.

3. The conditions depicted in Habakkuk 1:2-4 seem to describe the social, religious, and moral situation during the reign of Jehoiakim (609-597 B.C.).

Habakkuk gave his prophecy during the decline of the Assyrian

Empire and the emergence of the mighty Babylonian Empire. The Assyrian Empire ruled the Middle East during the seventh century B.C., but it met its end in 612 B.C. at the hands of Nabopolassar of Babylon and Cyaxares of Media. Assyria had virtually ceased to exist by the end of the century.

With the fall of the Assyrian Empire, political supremacy in the area belonged to Egypt. By 608 B.C., Pharaoh-neco had defeated Judah and killed King Josiah. He allowed Josiah's son, Jehoahaz, to rule Judah, but his rule lasted only three months. Pharaoh-neco replaced Jehoahaz with another of Josiah's sons, Jehoiakim, who also proved to be a wicked ruler. In 605 B.C., Nebuchadnezzar of Babylon defeated Pharaoh-neco and his army at Carchemish and, in the process, pursued them to Judah. It was during this time that Nebuchadnezzar subdued Jerusalem and took captive thousands of Judah's young men, including Daniel.

Jehoiakim was killed when he rebelled against the Babylonian occupation. Upon his death, his son Jehoiachin was placed in power. After ruling only three months, Jehoiachin was carried off to Babylon with 10,000 Judeans in 597 B.C., and Zedekiah was made king over Judah. After ruling nearly ten years, he too rebelled against the Babylonian occupation. It was at that time (586 B.C.) that the Babylonians destroyed Jerusalem and Solomon's Temple, leaving only a remnant of people under the rule of Gedaliah, the governor.

During this period in Judah's turbulent history, God answered Habakkuk's probing questions and revealed the nation's destiny. In chapter 1, Habakkuk dialoged with God over His seeming indifference to Judah's wickedness. When God revealed His judgment of Judah's sin, Habakkuk expressed his displeasure over God's use of the wicked Babylonians to bring judgment on His people. In chapter 2, Habakkuk patiently sat back to wait and watch for God's answer to his dilemma. God revealed that He would use the Chaldeans as a rod to chasten Judah, but their ruth-lessness and corruption would be self-destructive, bringing about their own ruin (2:6-19). Habakkuk learned that evil never suc-ceeds, for the wicked are eventually destroyed, "but the just shall live by his faith" (2:4) and survive the tyrant's onslaught. In chap-ter 3, Habakkuk broke forth in prayer, petition, and praise, having understood God's sovereign plan on behalf of Judah's chastening and its enemies' destruction.

Habakkuk 1:1-4

The burden which Habakkuk, the prophet, did see. O LORD, how long shall I cry, and thou wilt not hear! Even cry out unto thee of violence, and thou wilt not save! Why dost thou show me iniquity, and cause me to behold grievance? For spoiling and violence are before me; and there are those who raise up strife and contention. Therefore, the law is slacked, and justice doth never go forth; for the wicked doth compass about the righteous; therefore, justice goeth forth perverted.

WHERE IS THE GOD OF JUSTICE?

Sick society is a phrase often used to describe the moral degeneracy in American culture. Analyses warn that the tidal wave of moral changes sweeping this country could mean the collapse of its social order.

Sick art forms portray distorted freak figures of despair. Sick music blares out weird vibrations arousing the sensual emotions of its listeners and resulting in dehumanizing acts. Sick commercials on television advertise the latest movies filled with crime, violence, drugs, sex, and demonic acts of horror. Much more could be said about the destructive forces of the sexual revolution, New Age movement, Eastern religious cults, and occult philosophies gaining acceptability throughout the country.

Many concerned Christian leaders have stepped forward to be

voices of hope. They have formed movements and legal organizations to fight the tide of moral decay that is eroding society.

None of this is new! In Habakkuk's day, Judah had become rotten to the core. It was ripe for judgment, but judgment was not forthcoming. Like many leaders today, Habakkuk was a voice attempting to stem the tide of moral decay eating away at Judah. Like many today, he wondered why God allowed wickedness to prevail without bringing judgment. Thus, Habakkuk had a dialogue with God over the problem of justice.

CONCERN OVER JUSTICE

Habakkuk's concern was expressed in the phrase, "The burden which Habakkuk, the prophet, did see" (v. 1). Three ideas are presented in this short introduction to show the prophet's heartfelt concern about the nation's condition.

Habakkuk's name means *embrace.* How appropriate, for although he was concerned that God's justice prevail over Judah's sin, he would *strongly embrace* them to his heart (as one would a wayward child), hoping that through love and compassion, they would acknowledge their sinful ways and return to God.

Habakkuk's concern became a "burden" (v. 1). The word *burden* has the idea of something heavy, a load to be lifted. He was burdened about the nation's sin and God's seeming indifference to act in judgment. But the message of judgment he had to deliver became a great burden as well.

Habakkuk "did see" (v. 1) the social, political, and religious evils of Judah. The woes pronounced against the Babylonians applied to Judah as well. Abusive leaders filled their coffers with ill-gotten gain (2:6-8), extorted from the poor (2:9-11), built cities at the price of human life (2:12-14), used drink to coerce people into lasciviousness (2:15-17), and committed idolatry (2:18-20).

What believer, if asked, could not articulate the same corruption in his or her own society? What believer, if asked, would not agree that more should be done to curb, correct, and stamp out that corruption? But what believer, if asked, would embrace his or her society in love, lift the burdensome message, and help correct the corruption? Few indeed! Not so with Habakkuk, for his concern broke forth into a cry for God to act.

CRY FOR JUSTICE

Although Jeremiah is known as the *Weeping Prophet*, Habakkuk, his contemporary, must be placed alongside him. The pent-up message of justice burning in his soul broke forth: "O LORD, how long shall I cry, and thou wilt not hear!" (v. 2). He had lamented over Judah's sin for a long time before he verbalized his burden.

The word *cry* is used twice in verse 2, each use having a different meaning. The first *cry* (*Shawa*) was for *help*. Habakkuk was asking how long he would have to wait until God sent an answer to his plea for help.

Jeremiah and Isaiah asked the same question, but David's cry for help was the most poignant. In Psalm 13, he asked, *How long?* four times in his plea for help: "How long wilt thou *forget me*, O LORD? Forever? How long wilt thou *hide thy face* from me? How long shall I *take counsel* in my soul, having sorrow in my heart daily? How long shall *mine enemy be exalted* over me?" (vv. 1-2, italics added). Although the heavens were silent, David came to the place where he trusted God for the answer to his *How long?* He trusted in the "mercy" (loving-kindness) of God (v. 5), knowing that He had a purpose for His delay. He had faith in God's "salvation" (v. 5), believing that He would not allow his enemy to triumph over him. He was able to "sing unto the LORD" (v. 6) in the midst of trial because of God's bountiful help in past times of distress. Faith kept David from withering under oppressing trials by bringing to remembrance former victories of God's power, mercy, and faithfulness to him. By reflecting on David's experience, Habakkuk could be greatly encouraged and supported through God's purposeful delay.

The second word for *cry* (*Zaag*) is a more intense cry for help, meaning a *shout* or *scream.* God's silence toward the prophet's prayer caused him to scream out a fervent cry for justice against the violence in Judah.

The "violence" (v. 2) being experienced in the land was extreme, similar to that manifested before the flood (Gen. 6:13). People had become totally corrupt and oppressive to each other, for "every imagination of the thoughts of his heart was only evil continually" (Gen. 6:5).

Only a generation earlier, King Josiah had purged Judah of Baal worship. He had the priests who served Baal burned on their own altars, which were then torn down, the images broken in pieces, ground to dust, and scattered over the graves of those who worshiped them (2 Chr. 34:4-5).

Josiah not only destroyed idol worship, he repaired the Temple and restored its worship. While the Temple was being repaired, Hilkiah the priest discovered the law and read it to the king, who immediately repented of his sin and required that the nation do likewise.

King Josiah died at the hand of Pharaoh-neco, king of Egypt. Josiah's son, Jehoahaz, succeeded him in rule, but Pharaoh-neco dethroned him after a reign of only three months (2 Ki. 23:31-33).

Pharoah-neco replaced Jehoahaz with another of Josiah's sons, Eliakim, who later changed his name to Jehoiakim. Jehoiakim was a godless, dictatorial despot who raped the people of any wealth they had left after Pharaoh-neco had impoverished them by extorting great amounts of tribute.

Jehoiakim went on to build a huge regal palace—paneled with expensive cedar, painted in vermilion, and studded with jewels—at both the forced and unpaid labor of his subjects.

Religiously, he undid all the reforms of his father Josiah. He raised up shrines of worship in Jerusalem and introduced many heathen gods and religious practices from Egypt. The epitome of his contempt toward God was when he cut into pieces and burned the scroll from Jeremiah detailing the catastrophic judgment that was about to descend on him and the land (Jer. 36:1-26).

His reign can be summed up in the words of Jeremiah: "But thine eyes and thine heart are not but for thy covetousness, and for shedding innocent blood, and for oppression, and for violence, to do it" (Jer. 22:17). Jeremiah went on to predict that Jehoiakim would not be lamented in death, nor buried, but dragged outside of the city and dumped on the garbage pile of Jerusalem (Jer. 22:18-19; 36:30). He was humiliated in death because he committed the horrible sins of Manasseh, filling Jerusalem with innocent blood (2 Ki. 24:3-4).

Although reform did take place in Judah, it was short-lived, for the leaders turned back to the old ways of polluting the land, perverting the people, and provoking the Lord to judgment.

Habakkuk screamed as fervently as he knew how against the moral depravity of his day, but God remained silent.

COMPLAINT ABOUT JUSTICE

The cry of Habakkuk's *How long?* progressed into the complaint of *Why? God, why don't You bring judgment in the midst of such iniquity and violence? God, why do You remain silent to my fervent prayers?* Habakkuk was perplexed because it was out of character for a holy God to behold sin (1:13) and not judge it.

Puzzled over God's silence, Habakkuk asked, "Why dost thou show me iniquity, and cause me to behold grievance? For spoiling and violence are before me; and there are those who raise up strife and contention" (v. 3). He was saying, *God, if You refuse to act or answer prayer, why do You show me the depths of Judah's depravity?*

Habakkuk used six descriptive words to express the moral decay surrounding him. Judah was full of "iniquity," which emphasized the physical trouble or corruption in the nation. Iniquity leads to "grievance" or distress suffered by people who are exploiting their neighbors for personal gain. When people are exploited, "violence" breaks out, resulting in the "spoiling" or destruction of government, home, and other social institutions. When self-serving, greedy individuals desire to do what is right in their own eyes, at the expense of others, "strife and contention" result.

Little has changed in 26 centuries! Like a modern Judah, the United States is sowing the seeds of moral decadence. On any given day there is a rape every 8 minutes, a murder every 27 minutes, a robbery every 78 seconds, a burglary every 10 seconds, and a car theft every 33 seconds.[1]

The divorce rate in this country has reached epidemic proportions, having risen 700 percent since the turn of the century. At present, there is one divorce for every 1.8 marriages. At least one million children per year must face the problem of their parents' divorcing. An overwhelming 38 percent of the children in America today will be reared by one parent.[2]

Is it any wonder that there are 450,000 adolescent alcoholics, while at least one-quarter of high school students get drunk at least once a month? Is it any wonder that one million teenage girls (1 out of 10) get pregnant each year, and 50 percent of the nation's 15- to 19-year-old girls have had premarital sex?[3] Is it any wonder that the number one criminal is a young person between the ages of 15 and 20 years old? Is it any wonder that drug abuse is costing the country between $10 and $17 billion annually and is responsible for more than 15,000 deaths per year? Is it any wonder that in 1996, in the public schools of this country, there were 200 murders, 6,000 robberies, 9,000 rapes, 20,000 assaults, and more than $600 million in property damage?[4]

What can account for the eroding moral fiber of young people in America? There are many factors, to be sure, but television has played a major role. By the age of 16, most children have watched between 10,000 and 15,000 hours of TV. Every hour of prime-time programming contains an average of five acts of violence. On the weekend, violent acts per hour on children's programs jump to 18.[5] Researchers have found that children are being impacted through television and are becoming more violent, aggressive, fearful, and less intelligent.[6] Is it any wonder that the United States faces so many social ills?

COMPLACENCY OF JUSTICE

Habakkuk came to a number of conclusions about justice in Judah. First, "the law is slacked" (v. 4), or paralyzed, because it had been ignored as a body of rules to govern the civil, moral, and religious life of the nation. The second conclusion flows naturally from the first. If the law is ignored, "justice doth never go forth" (v. 4). Because the law was not upheld by those called to administer it, the law was ineffective to bring about change in Judah. Habakkuk's next conclusion was that the righteous suffer under such conditions, for "the wicked doth compass about the righteous" (v. 4). He saw the righteous hemmed in and defrauded by wicked judges who had stripped them of their personal and property rights. Thus, the righteous had no redress to obtain justice. When justice was handed down, his final conclusion was that it "goeth forth perverted" (v. 4). The leaders had interpreted the law to distort its true meaning for their own gains. No wonder a righteous man such as Habakkuk, in his concern over sin, cried out to God, complaining about the complacency of justice.

Many people, like Habakkuk, are perplexed with the prosperity of the wicked who seem to flourish, while the faithful pine away under persecution. Asaph was one who became envious of the wealthy wicked. In Psalm 73, he portrayed the wicked as prosperous, proud, and perverted, persecuting the righteous with continual oppression. From the outside they did not seem to be plagued like other men, for they died in physical strength, without pain (Ps. 73:3-12).

Many of God's people are like Asaph, living in a society full of perverted laws and run by polluted leaders. They become discouraged about the seeming indifference and inactivity of God to bring change; thus, they themselves slip into an attitude of indifference and inactivity.

But Asaph took his perplexity to God and was shown the true end of the wicked (Ps. 73:17). From God's viewpoint, things are quite different for the wicked. They live in a slippery place, having no guarantee of their place and prosperity in society. Then they suddenly perish into perdition by means of terror (Ps. 73:18-19). Such was the case with Jehoiakim, who ruled at that time.

Asaph came to the realization that faith in God's sovereign control over the destiny of people and nations promised the only security (Ps. 73:21-28), even when God was silent to society's sufferings.

Although God's silence to the prophet's plea pictured Him as indifferent because of His inactivity, God neither slumbers nor sleeps (Ps. 121:4), as will be shown in the next chapter.

Remember, God's justice may work in mysterious ways, but He always has the answers to *How long?* and *Why?*

Habakkuk 1:5-11

Behold among the nations, and regard, and wonder marvelously; for I will work a work in your days, which ye will not believe, though it be told you. For, lo, I raise up the Chaldeans, that bitter and hasty nation, which shall march through the breadth of the land, to possess the dwelling places that are not theirs. They are terrible and dreadful; their judgment and their dignity shall proceed from themselves. Their horses also are swifter than the leopards, and are more fierce than the evening wolves; and their horsemen shall spread themselves, and their horsemen shall come from far; they shall fly like the eagle that hasteth to eat. They shall come all for violence; the set of their faces is forward, and they shall gather the captives as the sand. And they shall scoff at the kings, and the princes shall be a scorn unto them; they shall deride every stronghold; for they shall heap dust, and take it. Then shall his mind change, and he shall pass over, and offend, imputing this his power unto his god.

GOD'S UNBELIEVABLE WORK

God, where is justice? Why are You insensitive, indifferent, and inactive to the cry of the righteous? How long will You remain silent? cried Habakkuk, as he sat overwhelmed by the social and moral corruption flooding the land.

Insensitive? Indifferent? Inactive? Not God! Although it might seem as if He were a sleeping sovereign, God was very much awake and engaged in the affairs taking place in the Middle East.

God always has an answer to the plight, plea, and prayer of the righteous, but not always the answer the righteous expect. So it was with Habakkuk. God put forth an incredible answer to his prayer that left the prophet perplexed.

THE CHALDEANS CHOSEN

God is full of surprises for His people. Habakkuk was about to have his eyes opened to the full-orbed program that the Lord had planned for Judah.

First, Habakkuk was made aware of God's *world* involvement: "Behold among the nations" (v. 5). The Lord wanted him to see the big picture—have a world view—for the prophet and people were to understand that God controls every event among the nations of the world. As the song writer has penned, "He's got the whole world in His hand." Not only was Habakkuk to see it, he was to "regard" (v. 5) or *weigh well* what God was doing.

What was God doing? He had raised the Chaldeans to great power. They were a Semitic people tracing their history back to Nahor, the brother of Abraham (Gen. 22:23). The Chaldeans settled in the area known as Babylon; thus, they were called Babylonians. Nabopolassar, king of Babylon, was on the move in Habakkuk's day. He had destroyed the powerful Assyrian Empire (612 B.C.), which ruled the Middle East in the seventh century B.C. Nebuchadnezzar (son of Nabopolassar) had defeated Pharaohneco and his army at Carchemish (605 B.C.) and was now closing in on Jerusalem.

Is God inactive and indifferent to injustice? No! God was saying to the prophet, *If I have intervened in the affairs of the nations, will I do less with My people Judah? Surely not!*

Many Christians do not have a world view. They suffer from spiritual myopia. We must extend our sight globally and see the Lord's involvement. Justice does prevail as God raises up one nation and puts down another.

With social and moral corruption going unchecked in the United States today, many are asking, *Why hasn't God judged the nation?* It must be remembered that the wheels of God's justice grind slowly, but they keep on grinding. In His punitive righteousness, God must and will act upon the nation if repentance is not forthcoming. God has raised up powerful nations, like the Babylonians, who are on the move today and could bring a death-blow to the United States if He so allows. Christians can learn from Habakkuk's experience. God acts with a world view in mind.

Second, Habakkuk was made aware of the *wonder* of God's involvement: "Behold...and wonder marvelously" (v. 5). The words *wonder marvelously* literally mean *be amazed, be amazed.* When God revealed to Judah the way in which He would judge the nation's sin, both the prophet and the people would be shocked into disbelief. It would be so startling that they would "not believe, though it be told" to them (v. 5). They just could not believe that God would allow them to be destroyed by the heathenish Babylonians. Jeremiah echoed the same disbelief by the people: "They have denied the LORD, and said, It is not he; neither shall evil come upon us; neither shall we see sword or famine" (Jer. 5:12).

Prophet after prophet proclaimed that judgment was coming to a particular generation, but few ever believed it. Noah's generation did not believe it until the flood swept them away. Lot did not believe it until fire and brimstone were rained on Sodom and Gomorrah. The ten tribes did not believe it until the Assyrians destroyed them. During this age, people do not believe that the earth will suffer from God's judgment.

If asked today, many people would not believe that God will allow the United States to be leveled because of its sin. For some reason, there are those who see this country as a chosen people, privileged above others, one that cannot be touched with God's judgment. But remember, God will judge a sinful nation. World history bears that out.

When Paul preached in the synagogue at Antioch, he applied

Habakkuk's prophecy as a warning to those who would reject the Messiahship of Jesus (Acts 13:41). Paul's quote was altered somewhat because he used the Septuagint translation. Neither was he using the quote as a fulfillment of Habakkuk 1:5, but simply as an analogy. Through unbelief, the Jews in Paul's day were positioned for the same type of judgment as those whom Habakkuk had warned (Acts 13:40).

What was the judgment in Habakkuk's day? The Chaldeans would completely destroy Judah. The destruction of Jerusalem by the Chaldeans in 586 B.C. was a foreshadow of the Roman destruction in 70 A.D. By divine appointment, on each occasion Jerusalem and the Temple were destroyed on the same day—the ninth of Av (Tisha B' Av).

Paul not only applied the prophecy physically, but spiritually as well, referring to the destruction of eternal damnation that will come upon all who reject Jesus, both Jew and Gentile.

Third, Habakkuk was made aware of God's *work*, which would be incredible: "I will work a work in your days" (v. 5). What was the work? God would "raise up the Chaldeans...which shall march through the breadth of the land" (v. 6) and destroy Judah. When the Lord spoke of raising up the Chaldeans, it was not with reference to their coming forth as a world power; they had been that for 20 years. God was referring to the Chaldeans being raised up specifically to bring judgment on Judah.

Notice, it is God who raises up nations for His own power. Although God allows nations to become world powers, He has no part in their ungodly character or actions. He simply allows their evil propensities to be manifested for the purpose of judgment.

The Chaldeans would be "bitter" (fierce and cruel), and "hasty" (moving rapidly with impetuousness), and would "march through the breadth of the land, to possess the dwelling places that are not theirs" (v. 6).

Although God revealed His plan to raise up the Chaldeans, He did not give any reason for His choice or action. Why? For three reasons.

1. An infinite God is under no obligation to explain His actions to a finite creation. God's dealing with Job is a classic illustration. Although God allowed Job to go through intense suffering and to question his experience, He never fully explained His purpose for doing so (Job 38-42). God is sovereign and can do with His creation whatever He desires. This is seen in His dealing with Israel (Rom. 9-11). It must be remembered that God does all things right (Rom. 11:33-36).

2. God's thoughts and ways are different from those of mankind: "For my thoughts are not your thoughts, neither are your ways my ways, saith the LORD. For as the heavens are higher than the earth, so are my ways higher than your ways, and my thoughts than your thoughts" (Isa. 55:8-9). People, on their own, will never understand God's actions apart from His Word.

3. God did not give any reason for His actions because the plan was so unbelievable that the prophet and the people would refuse to believe it when they were told (v. 5).

A modern-day parallel to the impending brutal invasion by Babylon is the Holocaust of World War II. Many ask, *How could a loving God allow six million Jewish people to perish at the hands of Nazi brutality?*

Although judgment for disobedience was predicted for the Jewish people centuries before, the horrors of the 1933-1945 Holocaust, if told to the people, would have been unforeseeable, incomprehensible, and unbelievable. In fact, at the beginning of the Holocaust, many Jews in Europe felt no imminent danger of mass persecution, although Hitler harassed and intimidated them severely.

People have debated the Holocaust for more than 50 years without arriving at a satisfactory explanation as to why it was permitted to occur. There is no answer that will satisfy, apart from a biblical explanation.

It must be remembered that whatever happens to mankind, God is sovereignly in control of His creation and does all things perfectly, even though people cannot understand His actions. It must be remembered that people are limited in their perception and see only a few frames in the total picture of God's program. But the Lord knows the whole story, seeing it from beginning to end. It must be remembered that "The secret things belong unto the LORD our God" (Dt. 29:29). Moses was saying that people should have a settled faith in God, even though He chooses not to reveal the reasons for all of His actions. It must be remembered that God does not work in the time and manner of our expectations. Such was the case with Judah.

THE CHALDEANS' CHARACTER

The Chaldeans manifested *savage characteristics.* They are described as being "terrible and dreadful" (v. 7) because they were devoid of mercy or compassion. One writer is very descriptive as he portrays the barbarities that they poured out on their enemies. He writes,

> Just one paragraph is needed to show their savagery....Assurnatsipal's cruelties were especially revolting. Pyramids of human heads marked the path of the conqueror; boys and girls were burnt alive or reserved for a worse fate; men were impaled, flayed alive, blinded, or deprived of their hands and feet, or their ears and noses, while the women and children were carried into slavery,

the captured city plundered and reduced to ashes, and the trees in its neighborhood cut down....How deeply seated was the thirst for blood and vengeance on an enemy is exemplified in a bas-relief which represents Assurbanipal and his queen feasting in their garden while the head of the conquered Elamite king hangs from a tree above. What the Assyrians had previously been, the Chaldeans subsequently became, and this was the nation that God was raising up as His instrument of judgment.[1]

The most powerful armies melted away at their awesome strength and inhumanity. Habakkuk said, "their judgment and their dignity shall proceed from themselves" (v. 7), meaning that the Babylonians were a law unto themselves. They recognized the power of no other nation or other political system but their own. Nebuchadnezzar is a clear example of this, for his word was law. He was the highest in the land, and he recognized no god but himself, until the Lord humbled him (Dan. 4).

The Chaldeans were *swift in conquest.* The swiftness with which they would descend upon Judah is described in animalistic terms.

1. "Their horses also are swifter than the leopards [panthers]" (v. 8). No animal is more swift in attacking than the bloodthirsty panthers, whose feet barely touch the ground as they dart toward their prey.

2. They were "more fierce than the evening wolves" (v. 8). Wolves deprived of food comb vast areas looking for a meal at great risk to their lives.

3. "Their horsemen shall come from far; they shall fly like the eagle that hasteth to eat" (v. 8). The eagle (a great vulture), with keen sight, circles high above its prey waiting for the proper time to swiftly strike and snatch it.

No wonder the Judeans were terrified at the news that God was sending the Babylonians. Yet Moses had predicted it centuries earlier (Dt. 28:49-50).

No wall, gate, or city was impregnable to the Babylonians: "they shall deride every stronghold; for they shall heap dust, and take it" (v. 10). Laughing at the defenses of the enemy, the Babylonians simply built mounds of dirt against the city walls and besieged it (Ezek. 26:7-14).

The Chaldeans would *secure* and *scorn their captives.* They came for one reason—"violence" (v. 9)—which they thrived on. After their victory, "they shall gather the captives as the sand" (v. 9).

The king of Babylon would scoff and scorn (v. 10) the leaders whom he conquered and then make sport of them. The captured king and princes were caged like animals, after which the people mocked and ridiculed the monarch. Then he was decapitated. Similar treatment was suffered by King Jehoiakim, who was bound in fetters and carried off to Babylon during the first deportation of Judah (2 Chr. 36:6).

The Chaldeans had a *sweeping conquest* of the Middle East. After the Babylonian conquest of Judah, "Then shall his mind change [lit., then he shall sweep on like the wind], and he shall pass over, and offend [be guilty], imputing this his power unto his god" (v. 11). Although this verse seems difficult to interpret, God is simply saying that the Chaldeans, like a strong wind, would sweep away all that was before them. But because they used such inhumane treatment against the people they had conquered, their cup of "guilt" was being filled up before God, who would eventually judge them.

The Chaldeans did not impute "this his power unto his god" (v. 11) for victory over the Middle East, but praised their own might and ability as the source of victory. This was exactly what Nebuchadnezzar claimed for himself (Dan. 4:30). He claimed that his own strength was his god, a pattern that will be followed by the Antichrist when he comes on the scene (Dan. 11:37-38).

Such was the answer to Habakkuk's prayer. Often Christians pray, *God, where is justice? Do something about the moral and social corruption flooding the United States.* But what if God were to reveal how He was going to right the wrongs in this country? He is full of surprises. It might mean the demise of America. His answer to Habakkuk's prayer meant Judah's demise!

It is imperative that people pray for the right leadership for their country—leaders who will look to God for answers and seek to bring the nation to spiritual renewal before a modern-day Chaldean appears on the horizon with winds of judgment.

Habakkuk 1:12-2:1

Art thou not from everlasting, O LORD, my God, mine Holy One? We shall not die. O LORD, thou hast ordained them for judgment; and, O Mighty God, thou hast established them for correction. Thou art of purer eyes than to behold evil, and canst not look on iniquity; why lookest thou upon them that deal treacherously, and holdest thy tongue when the wicked devoureth the man that is more righteous than he? And makest men as the fish of the sea, as the creeping things, that have no ruler over them? They take up all of them with the hook; they catch them in their net, and gather them in their drag; therefore, they rejoice and are glad. Therefore, they sacrifice unto their net, and burn incense unto their drag, because by them their portion is fat, and their food plenteous. Shall they, therefore, empty their net, and not spare continually to slay the nations? I will stand upon my watch, and set myself upon the tower, and will watch to see what he will say unto me, and what I shall answer when I am reproved.

WATCHING FOR GOD'S ANSWER

Perplexed had to be Habakkuk's feeling when God answered his cry for justice in Judah. Most likely he sat in stunned silence, contemplating the unexpected revelation from God. The thought may have flashed across his mind, *How can a holy God tolerate the Chaldeans' sin, let alone use them to bring judgment upon Judah?* Judah, although sinful, was less wicked than the Chaldeans. It was all an enigma to Habakkuk, so inconsistent was the revelation with God's nature. Had he in some way misunderstood the message and means by which Judah would be chastened?

Misunderstood? No! Habakkuk had received the right message. God would use the Chaldeans, a sinful and savage people, to chasten Judah.

How would Habakkuk respond to God's message? He began by

rehearsing the seeming paradox, questioning, *How can a holy God use a sinful nation to accomplish His righteous purpose?*

PERPLEXED OVER THE SUCCESS OF THE WICKED

Habakkuk's search for an answer to his perplexity began from a position of faith. He attempted to understand the Lord's dealing with Judah by logically reviewing four truths he knew about God's nature and character.

First, God is *eternal.* "Art thou not from everlasting [lit., *from before*]…?" (v. 12). God is eternal in the sense of His relation to time. He stands outside of time, having neither beginning nor end, for time came to be at the point of creation (Jn. 1:3) and has meaning only in relation to it. The Bible attests to the eternality of God. Abraham called Him the "everlasting God" (Gen. 21:33). Moses said, "from everlasting to everlasting, thou art God" (Ps. 90:2). Isaiah revealed God as the "high and lofty One who inhabiteth eternity" (Isa. 57:15). For God to be God, He, of necessity, must have always existed. Because God is infinite and exists outside of time, the past, present, and future are all one—the *now* to Him. Therefore, He had full knowledge of the Chaldeans' character and action against Judah.

Second, the prophet knew that his God was the *"Holy One"* (v. 12). Holiness refers to God's absolute separateness from any moral evil. It is the foremost attribute expressing God's nature. Israel well knew the attribute of God's holiness, for He revealed it through the Levitical law, the priesthood, the laws of purity, the Tabernacle worship, the sacrificial system, and the feast days.

Third, because God is holy, He is of "*purer eyes than to behold evil* [look upon with approval], and canst not look on iniquity" (v. 13). Habakkuk concluded that God could in no way be charged with or implicated in sinful acts.

Fourth, Habakkuk called God a *"Mighty God"* (v. 12), which literally means a *rock*, referring to His immutability (unchangeableness). Moses described God as "the Rock, his work is perfect; for all his ways are justice; a God of truth and without iniquity, just and right is he" (Dt. 32:4). Five times Moses referred to God as a "Rock" in Deuteronomy (32:4, 15, 18, 30, 31).

The word *rock* refers to God as a sure *foundation*, a stable *refuge* from which Israel could succor sustenance as they rested beneath its shadow when facing the storms of opposition.

Christ referred to God as the trustworthy rock upon whom all men should build their lives (Mt. 7:24-27). Paul described Christ as the "spiritual Rock" (1 Cor. 10:4) who followed and protected the children of Israel during their 40 years in the wilderness.

Habakkuk also realized that God had "ordained [appointed] them [Chaldeans] for judgment; and...established [founded] them for correction [to chasten His people]" (v. 12). Knowing all of this, the prophet cried out, "We shall not die" (v. 12). Habakkuk knew that God had chosen Israel to be a "special people unto himself" (Dt. 7:6), a people with whom He had made an eternal, unconditional covenant, which the Lord sealed with blood.

Having reviewed his solid faith in the glorious character of God's person and program as it related to His purpose for Israel, Habakkuk still struggled with the haunting question, *How can a holy God use a sinful nation to accomplish His righteous purpose?*

God is "of purer eyes than to behold evil, and canst not look on iniquity" (v. 13). Habakkuk was not saying that God could not see sin, for "all things are naked and opened unto the eyes of him with whom we have to do" (Heb. 4:13). But God cannot endure or approve the deeds of the wicked, for His holy nature would repel it—evil being the opposite of holiness.

Because God is holy and abhors sin, Habakkuk had two questions that needed answers. First, "why lookest thou upon them that deal treacherously...?" (v. 13). The prophet wondered why God would choose a beastly, heathenish people like the Chaldeans and bestow on them favor, honor, and prosperity. How could He use this people for any purpose, let alone to chasten Judah?

This invoked a second question from Habakkuk: "why...holdest thy tongue when the wicked devoureth the man that is more righteous than he?" (v. 13). The prophet could not understand how a holy God could keep silent and restrain from manifesting His justice against the wicked Chaldeans, for Judah, although wicked, was much more righteous than the Chaldeans.

On a humanistic level, Habakkuk's assumption might seem correct. Judah would be considered more righteous. But to say that Judah was more righteous than the Chaldeans was a misconception, for no person is righteous in God's sight. Habakkuk should have said, *the nation that sinned less before God.*

God was not chastening Judah on the basis of who was or was not the greater sinner—Babylon or Judah. Judgment was coming because Judah had refused to repent of its sin after years of warning. God remained silent to the prophet's questions.

God does not always answer the many questions that righteous people have, in the time or manner they desire. All believers have experienced times of delay or have received no answers to their questions. There is the cry of *Why?* from a husband and wife who could not have children, but the answer is not given. There is the cry of *Why?* when parents lose a child, but the answer is not given. There is the plaintive *Why?* of a paraplegic who has been debilitated by a freak accident, but the reason is never given. In Habakkuk's case, the answer would come, but not now.

PERMITTING THE WICKED TO SUCCEED

Still perplexed over God's ways, Habakkuk continued to question

Him about what was happening to Judah. He asked, wasn't Judah as "fish of the sea, as the creeping things, that have no ruler over them?" (v. 14).

Fish and creeping things are helplessly weak and unable to buck either the fierce waters or winds that push them along to their destruction. Even if they wanted to fight back, they have neither the physical nor the mental ability to cry for help. Having no power to resist their environment, they are at the mercy of whatever befalls them. Moreover, they have no leader to provide wisdom, protection, or guidance away from the predator that waits to destroy them. Such was the case in Judah—or any nation—when God removes His providential care.

The Chaldeans were a formidable predator against Judah, who took "up all of them with the hook...and gather[ed] them in their drag [net]" (v. 15). A similar revelation was given to Jeremiah. God said that after He sent the fishermen to net the Judeans, He would send for many hunters who would comb the mountains, hills, and cliffs of the rocks for captives (Jer. 16:16). None would escape captivity. This was graphically portrayed when the Romans defeated Israel in 70 A.D. They sought out every pocket of resistance.

Habakkuk was crying out in concern, *God, how can You allow Your people to be swept away in the net of captivity as insignificant creatures by such brutal beasts as the Chaldeans?* No answer ever came.

Nations should learn a number of lessons from Judah's experience. First, they should not boast in their strength, for their prosperity and power are from the Lord. If God chooses, He can remove them in a moment, without notice. Second, they should not rely upon their finite cunning, for they are at the mercy of God, who can sweep them away like fish and creeping things. Third, when the net of judgment falls, everything is swept away. The righteous are dragged off with the wicked.

PROMOTING THE WICKED

Another of Habakkuk's perplexities was the promoting of the Chaldeans, for they "sacrifice unto their net, and burn incense unto their drag" (v. 16). Instead of bowing the knee to the omnipotent God as the source of victory over the nations, they deified the power of their weapons and thus themselves (cp. v. 11). How could God prosper a nation who refused to credit Him for their victories?

Habakkuk questioned, "Shall they, therefore, empty their net, and not spare continually to slay the nations?" (v. 17). They had subdued nation after nation as fish (Assyria, Egypt, etc.), and now they were on the threshold of doing the same to Judah. Was there no stopping them? Would God just let them incessantly empty their net to fill it again with the spoils and slayings of the nations? Would God allow them to continually rejoice and be glad (v. 15) in their evil pursuits? Would God stand idly by as they lifted up the clenched fist, deifying the power of man?

A modern-day counterpart was the leadership of the former Soviet Union, who, in the past, were avowed atheists and worshiped the power of their state. Like a cancer, they swept across the world promoting revolutions, trying to gain a foothold in third world countries in order to subdue and eventually control them. They netted nation after nation, giving credit for their victories to their god, the Communist system.

PROPHET'S WATCH

Although Habakkuk knew that he had been rash and pointed in his questions to God, he would wait and watch, trusting Him for the answers. As a servant before his master, the prophet said, "I will stand upon my watch, and set myself upon the tower, and will watch to see what he will say unto me" (2:1).

Habakkuk did not become impatient and assertive, demanding

to know why God had acted as He did. Neither did he strike out against God, calling Him unjust in His dealings with Judah. Nor did he talk of giving up the faith, unable to believe in a God who would use the wicked to chasten His people. Instead, Habakkuk set himself upon the watchtower (not physically, but mentally), waiting to see (not hear) how God would answer him.

The prophet was not afraid of being reproved for his questions, as some versions seem to indicate. The words "when I am reproved" (2:1) are better translated, *when God argues with* [answers] *me.* He was simply saying that when God answered him, it would be in the form of an argument. Thus, while Habakkuk watched as a sentinel, he would contemplate the type of response to give when God revealed His answer.

Habakkuk knew that God is faithful. He would never forget, fail, falter, or forfeit His Word.[1] He knew that "God is not a man, that he should lie" (Num. 23:19). He knew that God must chasten Judah, but He would not remove His loving-kindness. His faithfulness to them would not fail (Ps. 89:32-33). Therefore, he would wait and watch to see how God would answer him.

A watchman must have the keen eye of an eagle, able to spot imminent danger. He must have nerves of steel and be steadfast in his assignment, not leaving his post for fear of an approaching enemy. He must be alert, for to sleep at his post could mean destruction for his people. To be selected as a watchman was a trusted honor, for the leadership of his country put the security of the nation in his care. Above all, a watchman was to be faithful to his commission. Unfaithfulness is unforgivable, for the result would be certain death for him and his people.

Habakkuk was this type of watchman—keen-eyed, seeing the imminent danger coming upon Judah. He had nerves of steel, willing to be steadfast in defense of his people, but questioning why God would allow such a wicked nation to destroy Judah. He was not asleep, but spiritually alert, ready to receive God's answer to his perplexity. Habakkuk knew that a watchman must be faithful to his commission, obedient to the voice of God, whether or not He responded to his dilemma.

Today, believers wonder why God allows certain things to take place in their lives. They cry out in prayer, only to find God silent to their requests.

Oswald Chambers has written, "God's silences are His answers....His silence is the sign that He is bringing you into a marvelous understanding of Himself....God has trusted you in the most intimate way possible, with an absolute silence, not of despair, but of pleasure, because He saw that you could stand a bigger *revelation*."[2]

In Habakkuk's case, it was the bigger *revelation* that God would give of Himself and His purpose for Judah, but he must patiently watch and wait for it. The same is true in the lives of believers today.

Chambers went on to say, "A wonderful thing about God's silence is that...His stillness gets into you and you become perfectly confident—'I know God has heard me.' "[3]

Many times believers do not understand what the Lord is working out in their lives, but they have the assurance that, although God may be silent, He is in control. May the words of our Lord to Peter—"What I do thou knowest not now, but thou shalt know hereafter" (Jn. 13:7)—undergird us in times when God is silent.

Habakkuk 2:2-4

And the LORD answered me, and said, Write the vision, and make it plain upon tablets, that he may run that readeth it. For the vision is yet for an appointed time, but at the end it shall speak, and not lie; though it tarry, wait for it, because it will surely come, it will not tarry. Behold, his soul that is lifted up is not upright in him; but the just shall live by his faith.

THE JUST SHALL LIVE BY FAITH

"Patience is a virtue, possess it if you can, seldom found in woman, and never in a man," wrote a perceptive person. There are those who would disagree—especially that women are somewhat patient but men never are. Nevertheless, society as a whole is very impatient.

Sit in a fast-food restaurant, stand in a slow-moving line at the bank, or get behind a creeping truck on a two-lane street, and people's impatience becomes very evident.

Many are spiritually impatient as well. Christians want instant answers to prayer, instant salvation of a loved one, instant healing of a terminal illness, or instant revelation of God's will for their lives. Who has not thought, *God, give me patience, but please hurry!*

Habakkuk was different. Although he sought answers to his perplexity concerning God's dealing with Judah, he was patient, for he said, "I will *stand...set* myself...to *see* what he [God] will say unto me" (v. 1, italics added). The prophet knew that God would answer him in time, so he waited, but not apathetically. Habakkuk watched eagerly for the revelatory answer from God.

REVELATION TO THE PROPHET

Habakkuk's patience was rewarded with a revelation from God: "And the LORD answered me, and said, Write the vision" (v. 2). The answer was presented in writing before the prophet's eyes. The word *vision* (Heb., *hazah*) means *perception* and is a supernatural visual revelation to a person while he or she is awake.

Habakkuk was to record the vision by legibly engraving it in large letters on a clay tablet so that everyone passing by could understand it.

The words, "that he may run that readeth it" (v. 2) have nothing to do with the message being placarded in a public place so that people jogging by could easily read it. If this were the case, Habakkuk would have written, *that the runner may read it.* The idea was that the one who read it would run to reveal the joyful news—that in God's time He would destroy Judah's enemy and deliver them from Gentile oppression.

RECORD OF THE PROPHET

Habakkuk was to commit the vision to writing for two reasons: so that others could read it, and to preserve its content because the fulfillment was yet future—"for an appointed time" (v. 3).

The phrase *appointed time* refers to the *divinely determined decree* of God, a specific period in His program. There was an appointed time when Judah's suffering for its sin would culminate (2:5-13, 15-19). There was an appointed time when Babylon would be destroyed by the Medo-Persian Empire (Dan. 5:25-31). This occurred on October 13, 539 B.C., when the Medo-Persians diverted the Euphrates River (which ran under the city walls) and entered the dried river beds of the city before the Babylonians knew what had happened. There is an appointed time that speaks of the future destruction of Gentile world rule at Christ's Second Coming (Rev. 17:1-20:3). Clearly, this vision has a prophetic fulfillment at Christ's coming by the way it is used in Hebrews 10:37. The writer of Hebrews (inspired by the Holy Spirit) changed the "it" (v. 3) to "he" (Heb. 10:37). Thus, "For yet a little while, and he [Christ] that shall come will come, and will not tarry" (Heb. 10:37). Christ will destroy Satan's diabolical world system, of which the Babylonians were a symbol in Habakkuk's day. During the Tribulation period, Babylon will again stand for the evil religious and political systems, like the Babylon of old. The political system will destroy the religious system, which in turn will be destroyed by Christ at His coming in glory.

Those reading the decreed vision were not to become *discouraged* concerning its lack of fulfillment in their day: "but at the end it shall speak" (v. 3). The word *speak* means to *breathe, pant,* or *hasten.* The truth in this vision is pictured as an animated, living word from God. The prophecy pants or hastens toward fulfillment, accomplishing, each step along the way, that which God desires for it.

Those reading the decreed vision were to understand that it will not *deceive*—"not lie" (v. 3) to them. When God utters a revelation, it will not be false nor will it fail, but it will come to fruition. God's veracity is seen in hundreds of prophecies that have already been fulfilled.

Those reading the decreed vision were not to be *disappointed by delay:* "though it tarry [linger], wait for it, because it will surely come, it will not tarry" (v. 3). To mankind, it seems as if God's

promised deliverance tarries, but the providence and purpose of
God do move toward fulfillment. They cannot be hurried, nor do
they linger, but move toward the appointed time of fulfillment.
Time is that way—it seems to move slowly. Yet we look back over
the years only to say how quickly they have passed.

Still, "The Lord is not slack concerning his promise, as some
men count slackness" (2 Pet. 3:9). To many people, it seems like
an eternity since the promise of Christ's Second Coming was
made nearly 2,000 years ago. But it must be remembered that
God's way of counting time differs from ours. We compare time
to time, whereas God sees time in the light of eternity. "One day
is with the Lord as a thousand years, and a thousand years as one
day" (2 Pet. 3:8).

A beautiful pattern for our walk with the Lord emerges in verse
3. First, there is God's *work* in the lives of believers. All of life has
its appointed time. Solomon well said, "To every thing there is a
season, and a time to every purpose under the heaven" (Eccl. 3:1; see
vv. 2-11). God promised that at the appointed time Sarah would
have the son of promise (Gen. 18:14). At the appointed time, God
provided Rebekah to be Isaac's wife (Gen. 24:14). At the appointed time, God brought a plague upon Egypt (Ex. 9:5). Job believed
that God directed in his time of trial and triumph when he wrote,
"For he performeth the thing that is appointed for me" (Job. 23:14).
Job also said, "Is there not an appointed time to man upon earth?"
(Job 7:1). Solomon echoed the same idea when he wrote that there
is an appointed "time to be born, and a time to die" (Eccl. 3:2). Not
only are there appointments in this life, but in the one to come as
well: "And as it is appointed unto men once to die, but after this
the judgment" (Heb. 9:27). Believers are born, live, and leave this
earth all by God's appointment.

Second, believers can rely on God's *Word* to guide them through
their earthly pilgrimages, for it will "not lie" (v. 3). David revealed

something about the Word of God that is almost incomprehensible: "thou hast magnified thy word above all thy name" (Ps. 138:2). The names of God stand for all that He is in His perfection, existence, attributes, wisdom, power, and unchangeableness. And yet He has magnified His Word above His name! In fact, believers can put more reliability on the Word of God than on the works of His hands. Jesus said, "For verily I say unto you, Till heaven and earth pass, one jot or one tittle shall in no way pass from the law, till all be fulfilled" (Mt. 5:18). Believers should take great encouragement from the Scriptures.

Third, believers must *wait* for the Lord's timing for things they desire in life. Dr. V. Raymond Edman has written in his book, *The Disciplines of Life*, "God's disappointments are His appointments, that God's delays are not His denials."[1] Unfortunately, few Christians live as if this were true.

Unlike Habakkuk, many believers are too impatient and unwilling to spend time waiting before God, seeking Him for answers to the *Why?* questions of His dealings in their lives. But many of the great servants of God waited in preparation for God to reveal His plan for them. Abraham waited 25 years for the promised son, Isaac. Joseph, sold into slavery, waited for years to understand why it was allowed, but he later said, "God did send me before you to preserve life" (Gen. 45:5). Moses spent 40 years in the desert of Midian waiting for the Lord to reveal His will to him. Christ spent 30 years in the obscure village of Nazareth waiting for the time of His ministry.

Dr. Edman put it well when he said, "Delay never thwarts God's purpose, it polishes His instrument....Delay does not forget God's servant nor cause His faithfulness to fail; rather, it fortifies their soul and vindicates His name....Delay that instructs and prepares saves time, never loses it."[2]

RIGHTEOUS PRINCIPLE

God answered Habakkuk's questions by setting forth a righteous principle. He showed the prophet that there are two types of people in the world. First, there are *sinners:* "Behold, his soul that is lifted up [puffed up with pride] is not upright in him" (v. 4). This passage refers to the wicked Chaldeans, who were a type of all mankind. Dominated by pride, people rebel against God, shutting themselves off from salvation.

King Nebuchadnezzar was the epitome of pride until God humbled him. His kingdom was taken from him, and he was driven into the wilderness. He lived there like a wild beast for seven years, until he acknowledged that God was the one who had dominion over kings and kingdoms. Nebuchadnezzar concluded that "those that walk in pride he [God] is able to abase" (Dan. 4:37).

Standing in contrast are *saved people,* represented by the believing Judeans: "but the just [righteous] shall live by his faith" (v. 4). Righteous people acknowledge their sinful state, humble themselves in repentance before God, and, having received forgiveness, are declared righteous. Habakkuk was not emphasizing *justification by faith,* as the verse is used in the New Testament, because in this context he began with the righteous person who had been justified.

The Hebrew language has no word for *faith.* The word translated *faith* in this passage is *emuna,* which means *firmness, faithfulness, fidelity.* This does not mean that Old Testament believers were not people of faith. Nor does it mean that they were not justified by faith, because Abraham "believed in the LORD; and he counted it to him for righteousness" (Gen. 15:6). When Abraham put his trust in God, God reckoned His own righteousness to him, counting him as a justified man.

The word translated *faith* denotes *faithfulness.* Justifying faith will manifest itself in faithful living before the Lord.

Herein is the answer to Habakkuk's perplexity. *Pride* is sin, which leads to death; whereas *faith* in God leads to justification (righteousness), producing life. The Judeans who exercised faith in God found Him faithful to bring future deliverance. But the proud Chaldeans, although they flourished for a while, carried seeds of sinful pride that brought them to destruction.

This verse is not only the theme of Habakkuk, it is a central passage for three New Testament epistles: Romans, Galatians, and Hebrews.

In Romans 1:17, the emphasis is on, "*The just* shall live by faith." The only people who can live by faith are just people. When sinners put their faith in the shed blood of Jesus Christ to take away their sin, God declares and treats them as justified; their sins are forgiven, and no charge can be laid against them (Rom. 8:1, 31-34). Closely connected to the term *justification* is the word *righteousness*. To justify someone is to declare that person legally righteous in God's eyes. Justified people have the imputed righteousness of Christ deposited in their lives. Thus, justified (righteous) people are able to live by faith. It is their faith (trust in God) that keeps them through times of adversity.

In Galatians 3:11, the emphasis is on, "The just *shall live* by faith." Paul quoted this verse to counter the Judaizers, who were teaching that people might be justified through faith, but to retain their salvation they must keep the law in their daily lives. Paul countered, *Not true.* People who are justified by faith live this principle of life too. People could never gain acceptance by the works of the law, for the law only condemned them. This was true even when Israel lived under the law, for God said to Habakkuk, "the just shall live by his faith." Thus, righteous people live by faith, not by keeping the legalistic system in the law.

In Hebrews 10:38, the emphasis is on, "the just shall live *by faith*." In this context, many of the Hebrew Christians, who had been justified by faith in Jesus Christ, considered turning back to their old Jewish religion because of persecution. The writer of Hebrews tried to fortify them for future trials by reminding them of how they originally exercised faith in Jesus as their Messiah. He encouraged them not to cast away their confidence in the Lord, for He would richly reward them in the future if they stayed true to the faith. They had to persevere until the Lord came, which would not be long (Heb. 10:35-37). If they denounced their faith in Christ and returned to Judaism, they would become apostates, bringing the Lord's disfavor upon them for the remainder of their lives. Quoting from Habakkuk 2:4, the writer showed that people who are truly justified by faith will *live by faith* (Heb. 10:38).

The writer of Hebrews gave further evidence of what it means to live by faith in chapter 11. There he described what true faith is and then illustrated his point from the lives of Old Testament men and women who lived by faith in the midst of severe persecution.

No one knew better what it meant to wait patiently by faith in prayer for God's appointed time than did Hudson Taylor. Dr. Edman wrote,

> Hudson Taylor knew the testing that tempers the steel of the soul. Invalided, home at twenty-nine after six years of intensive service in China, he settled with his little family in the east end of London. Outside interests lessened; friends began to forget; and five long hidden years were spent in the dreary street of a poor part of London, where the Taylors were "shut up to prayer and patience." From the record of those years it has been written, "Yet, without those hidden years, with all their growth and testing, how could the vision and enthusiasm of youth have been matured for the leadership that was to be?" Faith, faithfulness, devotion, self-sacrifice, unremitting labor, patient, persevering prayer became their portion and power, but more,

there is "the deep, prolonged exercise of a soul that is following hard after God...the gradual strengthening here, of a man called to walk by faith not by sight; the unutterable confidence of a heart cleaving to God and God alone, which pleases Him as nothing else can." As the years of obscurity progressed, "prayer was the only way by which the burdened heart could obtain any relief"; and when the discipline was complete, there emerged the China Inland Mission, at first only a tiny root, but destined of God to fill the land of China with gospel fruit.[3]

Believing friend, God has an appointed time in which He will reveal what He has for you in every situation of your life. But like Habakkuk, you must by faith say, "I will *stand...set* myself...to *see* what he [God] will say unto me."

WOE TO THE WICKED

History is punctuated with nations who spread themselves like a green bay tree and with imperial precision subjugated the world under their feet.

In verse 5, the Chaldeans are pictured as a proud man, totally given over to wine, who becomes intoxicated with power and greed that move him to roam the earth and swallow up nations at will. The Chaldeans' appetite for spoil was as insatiable "as sheol, and is as death" (v. 5), which cannot be satisfied. Inflamed with a consuming passion for greater spoil, they piled up nations and their wealth as people do plundered treasure.

The righteous were perplexed by the *Why?* of it all. Why does God seem to allow dictators to triumph over democracy? Why does He seem to allow the poor to suffer at the hands of the prosperous?

Habakkuk 2:5-20

Yea, also, because he transgresseth by wine, he is a proud man, neither keepeth at home, who enlargeth his desire as sheol, and is as death, and cannot be satisfied, but gathereth unto himself all nations, and heapeth unto himself all peoples. Shall not all these take up a parable against him, and a taunting proverb against him, and say, Woe to him that increaseth that which is not his! How long? And to him that ladeth himself with thick clay! Shall they not rise up suddenly that shall bite thee, and awake that shall vex thee, and thou shalt be for booty unto them? Because thou hast spoiled many nations, all the remnant of the peoples shall spoil thee, because of men's blood, and for the violence of the land, of the city, and of all that dwell therein.

Woe to him that coveteth an evil covetousness to his house, that he may set his nest on high, that he may be delivered from the power of evil! Thou hast plotted shame to thy house by cutting off many peoples, and hast sinned against thy soul. For the stone shall cry out of the wall, and the beam out of the timber shall answer it.

Woe to him that buildeth a town with blood, and establisheth a city by iniquity! Behold, is it not of the LORD of hosts that the peoples shall labor only for fire, and the nations shall weary themselves for nothing? For the earth shall be filled with the knowledge of the glory of the LORD, as the waters cover the sea.

Woe unto him that giveth his neighbor drink, that puttest thy wineskin to him, and makest him drunk also, that thou mayest look on their nakedness! Thou art filled with shame for glory; drink thou also, and let thy shame come upon thee; the cup of the LORD's right hand shall be turned unto thee, and shameful spewing shall be on thy glory. For the violence of Lebanon shall cover thee, and the spoil of beasts, which made them afraid, because of men's blood, and for the violence of the land, of the city, and of all that dwell therein.

What profiteth the carved image that its maker hath engraved it; the melted image, and a teacher of lies, that the maker of his work trusteth in it, to make dumb idols? Woe unto him that saith to the wood, Awake; to the dumb stone, Arise, it shall teach! Behold, it is laid over with gold and silver, and there is no breath at all within it. But the LORD is in his holy temple; let all the earth keep silence before him.

Why does He seem to allow the godless to triumph over the godly? Why is it allowed? For God's own purposes!

Although the world may stagger under the power of evil nations, God is still sovereignly in control. Secular history has proven that their prosperity is fixed, their power is short-lived, and their doom is sealed. Such was the destiny of Babylon, who held sway over the Middle East during the sixth century B.C.

God had raised up the Chaldeans, granted them power, and used them to judge Judah, but they abused their power and had to be punished.

Five woes were symmetrically pronounced against them in five stanzas (strophes) of three verses each. They were uttered not only by God, but by all the nations whom the Chaldeans had mercilessly oppressed.

WOE AGAINST ILL-GOTTEN INCREASE

The nations who had been oppressed by the Chaldeans took "up a parable...and a taunting proverb against him" (v. 6). In satirical riddles filled with double meaning, the nations made up taunting songs about the Chaldeans' brutality and their eventual judgment.

The first woe was against Babylon because he "increaseth that which is not his" (v. 6). The nations asked, *How long will these atrocities be permitted to continue?*

In denouncing Babylon, God portrayed them as deceptive money lenders who "ladeth [loads] himself with thick clay [heavy pledges or debts]" (v. 6) through taking spoils from the nations. The huge wealth amassed by the Chaldeans is pictured as a great burden of debt (with interest) that was owed to the conquered nations.

These nations would rise and collect the debt. Like a fierce viper, they would "bite" and "vex" (v. 7) the Chaldeans. The word *vex* means to *shake violently*, like a person would shake a debtor who refused to pay. God would turn the Chaldeans over to the nations as "booty" (v. 7) for the "blood" and "violence" (v. 8) done to them.

Individuals and nations think they are getting away with robbery in their wickedness to others, but they are simply piling up debts against themselves—and payday will come someday from the Lord. Sinners should not be deceived by thinking God does not see. People may forget, but God does not: "be sure your sin will find you out" (Num. 32:23). God is not to be mocked, for He has said, "whatever a man soweth, that shall he also reap" (Gal. 6:7).

WOE AGAINST INHUMANITY

The second woe was pronounced against the Chaldeans because of their covetousness, self-exaltation, and inhumanity. They are pictured as an eagle who builds its nest on a high mountain in order to be impregnable to predators (v. 9). The Chaldeans erected high walls and towers similar to those of Babel (Gen. 11:4) to protect themselves from invasion.

The plundered wealth collected by Nebuchadnezzar was to be used to build "his house" (v. 9) or dynasty. But he brought "shame" and retribution on his dynasty by inhumanely carrying "off many peoples" (v. 10) to work as slaves in building Babylon.

Even the inanimate "stone shall cry out of the wall, and the beam out of the timber shall answer it" (v. 11) because of the cruel slave labor practices of Nebuchadnezzar. Regardless of how strong or secure a people might be, whatever they build by covetousness or cruelty will witness against them and eventually cause their destruction. Such was the case soon after Nebuchadnezzar's reign.

Nebuchadnezzar's son, Amel Maruk (Evil Merodach; 2 Kings 25:27), reigned only two years (562-560 B.C.)

before he was assassinated by his brother-in-law, Nergal-Shar-Ussur, who ruled only four years. The latter's son, who succeeded him, was murdered nine months later. Nabonidus, one of the conspirators, seized power and appointed his son, Belshazzar, co-regent of Babylon, and under him the empire fell in disgrace (Dan. 5).[1]

Such was the case with the Edomites, who boasted of their strength and security (Obad. 3). But God said, "Though thou exalt thyself like the eagle...from there will I bring thee down" (Obad. 4).

Such was the case with the wealthy farmer who, coveting the so-called "good life" of ease and materialism, built bigger barns for his crops (Lk. 12:16-19). He died on the day of his decision, never to enjoy his wealth.

Such was the case with another rich farmer who, coveting his wealth, defrauded those who labored to bring in the harvest by refusing to pay them (Jas. 5:1-5). Money gained by inhumane practices will cry out in judgment against its owner. God has many ways of compensating evildoers. Often those who have built their empires on the blood of others die in ignominy, leaving their posterity a corrupted inheritance and a disgraceful name, or they lose the wealth altogether.

WOE AGAINST INIQUITY

The cup of iniquity was swiftly being filled by the Chaldeans, who built their city with "blood" and established it by "iniquity" (v. 12). They tirelessly built Babylon, using the riches of the people they had captured, and established the city through crime and tyranny. Daniel brought this problem to Nebuchadnezzar's attention when he interpreted his dream of the great tree (Dan. 4:26).

We cannot begin to imagine the exploitation of humanity in building Babylon.

> Superbly constructed, it spread over the area of fifteen square miles, the Euphrates River flowing diagonally across the city. The famous historian Herodotus said the city was surrounded by a wall 350 feet high and eighty-seven feet thick—extending thirty-five feet below the ground to prevent tunneling, and wide enough for six chariots to drive abreast. Around the top of the wall were 250 watchtowers placed in strategic locations. Outside the huge wall was a large ditch, or moat, which surrounded the city and was kept filled with water from the Euphrates River....Within this wall were one hundred gates of brass....The famous hanging gardens of Babylon are on record yet as one of the seven wonders of the world. Arranged in an area 400 feet square, and raised in perfectly cut terraces one above the other, they soared to a height of 350 feet. Viewers could make their way to the top by means of stairways, which were ten feet wide. Babylon was literally a city of gold (see Isa. 14:4). The city had fifty-three temples and 180 altars to Ishtar.[2]

But it was all built in vain: "Behold, is it not of the LORD of hosts that the peoples shall labor only for fire, and the nations shall weary themselves for nothing?" (v. 13). God had ordained that this gigantic fortified city was being built to become a huge bonfire (Isa. 50:11; Jer. 51:58). All the blood, sweat, and tears were for naught.

Habakkuk gave the reason for the emptiness of this humanistic project: "For the earth shall be filled with the knowledge of the glory of the LORD, as the waters cover the sea" (v. 14; see Isa. 11:9). No man-made kingdom will last for long, especially one built on the exploitation of others. Babylon, which was a type of all godless world powers, soon perished. Someday all godless kingdoms will be subdued at the return of the Messiah , when He breaks them into pieces. This prophecy looks forward to the Millennial Kingdom, when the glory and knowledge of the Lord will inundate every area of the world.

During the Kingdom, there will be no exploitation of individuals, but justice will permeate the world when the Lord rules in righteousness. Even the animals will not exploit each other, but will live in peace.

WOE AGAINST INTOXICATION

The Chaldeans were not only charged with oppressing the people, but with leading them into debauchery through drink. God said, "Woe unto him that giveth his neighbor drink, that puttest thy wineskin to him, and makest him drunk also" (v. 15). In verse 5, it was shown that the Chaldeans were totally given over to wine, which motivated them to roam the earth in brutal conquest. They also made the nations drink their wine, causing them to become mad (Jer. 51:7). Wine brought about the downfall of Babylon, for while the Chaldeans were in the midst of a drunken feast, the Medo-Persian Empire captured the nation (Dan. 5).

Drink was the major factor for many personal and social sins in Babylon. First, it produced *sexual sins*: "and makest him drunk also, that thou mayest look on their nakedness!" (v. 15). Alcohol lowers a person's inhibitions and often leads to immoral acts in which the person would not normally indulge.

This is illustrated in the account of Noah's drunkenness. Although Noah did not commit an immoral act while in his stupor, his son did. Ham, the father of Canaan, discovered his father lying naked in a drunken state and joked about it to his two brothers. He was judged severely for his deed (Gen. 9:20-27). The two brothers did not commit the same indecent act, but took a garment and walked backward to cover their father.

Second, drink manifested the Babylonians' *shame.* The nation had reveled in their shameful conduct, which, in God's sight, would only bring more disgrace upon them at their fall. They were commanded by God to drink and expose their own nakedness—"let thy shame come upon thee" (v. 16)—as they had done to their captives. This would be the epitome of degradation.

Third, drink produces *sickness:* "the cup of the LORD's right hand shall be turned unto thee, and shameful spewing shall be on thy glory" (v. 16). The Chaldeans were to drink the cup of God's wrath (Jer. 25:15, 27), which would come full circle from the nations upon them. They would begin to disgracefully vomit upon all their glory and would become a revolting sight to the world.

Fourth, drink produces great *squander.* The Chaldeans are pictured as inflicting devastation and waste on the resources of the nations they conquered: "For the violence of Lebanon shall cover thee, and the spoil of beasts" (v. 17). They wasted the cedars of Lebanon (Isa. 14:8) and caused fear to come upon the wild and domesticated animals that they destroyed. The same waste and fear would be inflicted upon them at their destruction.

The squander of both life and resources brought on by the use of alcohol in the United States staggers the imagination. Consider the following statistics.[3]

1. Nationally, alcoholism is the number three health problem, exceeded only by heart disease and cancer.

2. Every 20th alcoholic is a pre-teen; 3.3 million teenagers have a drinking problem.

3. More than 42 million children live in homes with alcohol-dependent parents, relatives, or guardians. Approximately 50 percent of those children will themselves develop a problem with alcohol.

4. Alcohol addicts outnumber drug addicts 10 to 1; alcohol-related deaths outnumber drug-related deaths 33 to 1.

5. Four out of every 10 hospital admissions, 50 percent of all auto fatalities, 55 percent of all arrests, 64 percent of all murders, and 60 percent of all child abuse cases are alcohol-related.

6. Medical studies show that an alcoholic's life expectancy is shortened by 10 to 12 years.

7. Every twenty-three minutes someone dies because of a drunk driver. One out of two Americans will be involved in an alcohol-related crash in their lifetimes. On any given Saturday night, 1 in 10 drivers on the highway will be legally drunk. Forty percent of all pedestrians killed are alcoholics.

Will things get better in the years to come? Probably not. No wonder the writer of Proverbs said, "Wine is a mocker, strong drink is raging, and whosoever is deceived thereby is not wise" (Prov. 20:1).

WOE AGAINST IDOLATRY

The woes against Babylon culminated in the greatest sin of all—idolatry. Habakkuk asked scornfully, "What profiteth the carved image that its maker hath engraved it…?" (v. 18). Clearly, no profit at all! These nonentities, which taught lies (v. 18), had no power for either good or evil. They were mere fabrications of mankind, utterly impotent to save Babylon from its doom.

Woe to the person who says to the dumb idol, "Awake...Arise, it shall teach!" (v. 19). *It shall teach?* cried Habakkuk. How could an inanimate piece of wood or stone, overlaid with gold and silver, possessing no breath (v. 19), teach when it could not speak? It could not!

In contrast to the dumb, inanimate idol, Habakkuk said, "But the LORD is in his holy temple" (v. 20). The true God is alive and seated on His heavenly throne in holiness, sovereignly in control of world events.

Unlike the idol, neither God nor His temple can be destroyed. Unlike the idol, He hears the cries and complaints of His people for justice. Unlike the idol, He has an answer for the perplexities of His people over life's situations. Unlike the idol, He will strike down the oppressor and bring about justice for the righteous.

Therefore, "let all the earth keep silence [hush] before him" (v. 20). What more need be said? Those who have sought the Lord for answers to their problems can wait in silent assurance, knowing that God will answer in His own time and in His own way. Thus it was with Habakkuk, who patiently waited to understand God's plan for judging a perverse people such as the Chaldeans. God will vindicate the righteous, for He said, "Vengeance is mine; I will repay, saith the Lord" (Rom. 12:19). Hush, my friend. God knows, and in time He will undertake for you as well.

Habakkuk 3:1-2

A prayer of Habakkuk, the prophet, upon Shigionoth. O LORD, I have heard thy speech, and was afraid; O LORD, revive thy work in the midst of the years, in the midst of the years make known; in wrath remember mercy.

REVIVE THY WORK, O GOD

While going through trying circumstances, people are often told, "Just pray about it. You know that prayer changes things!" We are left with the impression that God will alter the circumstances for good when prayer is offered in faith.

Does prayer really *change things*, in and of itself? Does God simply alter circumstances because people breathe their desires to Him in prayer? If God changes things because people pray, how does prayer fit into His sovereign will for the world? Does God's program for the world depend upon individuals' prayers? If God's will for the world is already fixed, what's the use of praying? If prayer does not change things, then it must be a futile charade and a waste of time. Such questions concerning prayer have plagued people for years.

Prayer is not a charade, nor is it a waste of time. Believers are to pray because God has commanded them to do so. Through prayer, believers can have a vital relationship with God through which they learn to know Him intimately, because prayer is one means through which God has chosen to accomplish His sovereign purposes in the world. Yet, it is not prayer that changes things, but God who changes things when prayer is offered in faith, desiring that His will be implemented in a specific situation. More than changing *things*, prayer changes *people*. They are brought into conformity with God's will. This was Habakkuk's experience as he sought God for answers to his situation.

In chapter 3, Habakkuk's prayer is more than a petition. It is a beautiful ode filled to overflowing with adoration and praise, thanksgiving and recollection of how God had dealt with Israel. Habakkuk's prayer is sublime in both its poetic concepts and diction. It ranks as one of the finest pieces of Hebrew poetry in the Old Testament.[1]

The prayer is composed of three major divisions.

1. There is Habakkuk's request for God to revive His work and temper His wrath (vv. 1-2).

2. The prophet presented a portrait of God's power as he reviewed His mighty acts through history (vv. 3-15).

3. Habakkuk pondered God's power and expressed faith in His purpose, although it might have meant adversity for him (vv. 16-19).

The chapter begins with a title: "A prayer of Habakkuk, the prophet, upon Shigionoth" (v. 1). Some scholars believe that chapter 3 was not written by Habakkuk, but his name is given as the author in verse 1.

The meaning of "Shigionoth" (v. 1) is uncertain. It seems to denote a dithyrambic song of great emotion and passion. Although chapter 3 is titled a prayer, it is actually a hymn of praise. Habakkuk, filled with great excitement, reeled back and forth praising God in triumphant song, as he contemplated the Lord's victory over Judah's enemies.

In verse 2, Habakkuk expressed three desires for God to fulfill what He had determined for Judah.

GOD'S WORD REVEALED

Habakkuk's prayer began, "O LORD, I have heard thy speech" (v. 2). With his spiritual ear, the prophet had received God's revelation concerning what He would do in answer to Habakkuk's request.

What were the request and the response? Habakkuk had questioned God's seeming inactivity and indifference to his prayer concerning the injustice taking place in Judah (1:1-4). In His answer, God revealed an unbelievable work that was to be performed. He would raise up the heathenish Chaldeans and use them to bring judgment on Judah (1:5-6).

God's answer left Habakkuk utterly stunned and perplexed. He questioned, *How could a holy God use a sinful nation to accomplish His righteous purpose against Judah?*

The prophet did not receive an immediate answer to his question. Thus, as a servant before his master, Habakkuk stood upon his watch to see how the Lord would answer him (2:1). He did not become impatient, demanding an answer. Neither did he strike out against God, calling Him unjust in His dealings with Judah. Nor did he talk of giving up the faith because God was going to use the wicked Chaldeans to chasten his people. Rather, he waited in prayer to receive God's answer (1:12-2:1).

Habakkuk's patience was rewarded by another revelation from God. At the *appointed time*, He would judge the Chaldeans. In the meantime, "the just [righteous] shall live by his faith" (2:4). He was to trust God, knowing that in His time He would manifest justice to all—both the Judeans and the Chaldeans (2:2-20).

Habakkuk had been humbled by the report of God's work. No more did he question God's dealings with Judah, for he knew that God would be just in that which His hand performed against them.

How was Habakkuk brought to a place of submission to God's plan? First, he took his eyes off of his surroundings—Judah's condition and the choice of the cruel Chaldeans to bring judgment. Second, he submitted his circumstances to God in prayer, trusting Him for an answer to his perplexity. Third, he patiently and alertly waited for a word from God concerning his request. Fourth, when the word was revealed, he accepted it and his perplexity vanished. The same pattern should be followed today by those who desire to know God's will during times of trial and uncertainty.

When Habakkuk heard God's Word, he "was afraid" (v. 2). He stood in *reverential awe* of what God was about to perform in judgment upon both Judah and Babylon. He had cried for justice, but when God revealed it, he was overwhelmed by its severity. The revelation affected his entire being, for he said, "When I heard, my belly [inner man] trembled, my lips [voice] quivered...rottenness [decay] entered into my bones [his legs became weak], and I trembled in myself" (v. 16). Other Bible figures—such as David , Isaiah, Jeremiah, Daniel, and John—were physically moved when hearing the Word of God or seeing the Lord's holiness. Few people today are so affected by God's prophetic truth.

GOD'S WORK REVIVED

Upon receiving God's word, Habakkuk prayed that His work would be revived: "O LORD, revive thy work in the midst of the years" (v. 2). Once he fully understood what God had planned for His people, Habakkuk petitioned the Lord to bring it about. To many people, this would seem like a strange petition, but the prophet desired that the Lord's will prevail.

The Hebrew word *revive* (*hayah*) means to *live, preserve,* or *keep alive.* It has nothing to do with the present-day concept of revival. In fact, the term *revival* is often misapplied today. Churches advertise in the media that revival meetings are to be held on certain dates, and the public is invited to hear both a famous evangelist and good gospel music. It is hoped that through prayer and evangelistic preaching, people will accept Christ, new life will be breathed into the church membership, and individual believers will rededicate their lives to the Lord. In such meetings, true revival can sweep over the congregation and produce a lasting commitment on the part of many believers. But, in all due respect, these meetings should be described as *evangelistic* meetings rather than revivals.

Many Christians confuse the concept of evangelism with revival. Evangelism is the spreading of Christ's gospel to a lost humanity. Revival is an extraordinary work of God whereby He brings a sinful believer to renewed spiritual life by means of the Holy Spirit's convicting power. Revival takes place when a few dedicated people earnestly pray for God to move on a church or a society. The longevity of a revival can vary. Some last a few days and others a few weeks, but the changes produced last for years.

American history is punctuated with revivals that usually came during times of moral declension or a longing for spiritual renewal. Revivals bring in their wake the salvation of many, mass rededication of Christians, commitment to missionary service, the building of new churches and Bible schools, and social reforms.

Habakkuk was not requesting that God revive Judah to a place of commitment, but he wanted God's *work* to be revived.

To what work was the prophet referring? God's predicted judgment that was to fall upon Judah at the hands of Babylon (1:5-6). Had Habakkuk always been in agreement with what God planned to do?

No, it was an enigma to him, but further revelation convinced the prophet that God's work was righteous and must proceed as planned.

Although the prophet knew that judgment must fall, he also knew that Judah would "not die" (1:12) or utterly perish from the earth. God had chosen Israel to be a "special people unto himself" (Dt. 7:6), a people with whom He had made an eternal, unconditional covenant and sealed it with blood.

Not only did Habakkuk want God's work to be revived, but he petitioned Him to "make [it] known" (v. 2) before the judgment was executed.   God desired this as well, for the prophet had been instructed to receive the vision and write it down (2:2) so that others could read it and spread the news. Hopefully, those who read it would repent before disaster fell.

Habakkuk had come to a number of conclusions. First, he could not pray for Judah's preservation from judgment because it was not God's will.   Second, a holy God must judge sin. Third, he knew that Judah's renewal could come only after cleansing had taken place. Fourth, his supreme concern must be for God's will to be accomplished. Fifth, God must preserve the nation through judgment because His covenant with Israel guaranteed it.

GOD'S WRATH RECOGNIZED

Although Habakkuk was in full agreement with God's work, he cried out in prayer, "in wrath remember mercy" (v. 2). The Hebrew word for *mercy* (*rahem*) speaks of God's *deep inner feeling of compassion and pity.*

God's mercy is frequently described in two ways. First, there is the binding relationship of God with His children. He looks upon believers as an earthly father would look upon his own children, having mercy and pity on them because he knows that they are weak.

Second, God shows mercy on those whom He chooses for His sovereign purposes. He said to Moses, "I will be gracious, and will show mercy on whom I will show mercy" (Ex. 33:19).

God's loving mercy is expressed in several ways. His unconditional election of Israel was an act of mercy. His forgiveness shown to them on the basis of repentance, when they deserved judgment, was also an act of mercy. His continuing preservation from judgment through the centuries, even though they refused to repent, was a further act of mercy.[2]

Although God had suspended His mercy for a season, allowing judgment to fall on Judah, Jeremiah realized that God had *in wrath remembered mercy*. With tears streaming down his face, the prophet looked over Jerusalem and saw the awesome destruction that Babylon had left in its wake. Every wall and home had been broken down; the Temple had fallen like a green hedge surrounding a garden; the bodies of both young and old filled the streets to overflowing (Lam. 2). The hunger was unbelievable: babies died from thirst; young and old alike combed the streets begging for a morsel of food; mothers even boiled their own children and ate them (Lam. 4).

Yet, in spite of all this, Jeremiah could pen, "It is because of the LORD's mercies that we are not consumed, because his compassions fail not. They are new every morning; great is thy faithfulness" (Lam. 3:22-23).

Jeremiah knew full well that God still loved His people, for they did not perish during the Babylonian invasion. The Hebrew word he used to express God's mercy is *hesed* (Lam. 3:22). In essence, the word means that God is *gracious*, and God is *love*. This is solid proof that God compassionately cared for His stricken and suffering people. He graciously loved them![3]

Another scholar has expressed that *hesed* speaks of God's *loyalty* to the covenant relationship He has with Israel.

For Jeremiah, the only reason any hope remained was that God's compassions failed not. The prophet stepped out of the dark rubble of a destroyed Jerusalem with renewed hope and proclaimed that God's mercies "are new every morning; great is thy faithfulness."

God has continually stretched out His hand of love and mercy to Israel. It was prophesied in the Palestinian Covenant that although Israel had sinned against God, He would show mercy to them, upon repentance, and would restore them to the land in the latter days (Dt. 30:1-3). God has a permanent father-son relationship with Israel that will never be broken.

Inspired by the words of Jeremiah, "great is thy faithfulness," Thomas O. Chisholm penned three stanzas to a hymn to which he gave that title. The first and third stanzas read:

> "Great is Thy faithfulness," O God my Father,
>   There is no shadow of turning with Thee;
> Thou changest not, Thy compassions, they fail not;
>   As Thou hast been Thou forever wilt be.
>
> Pardon for sin and a peace that endureth,
>   Thy own dear presence to cheer and to guide;
> Strength for today and bright hope for tomorrow,
>   Blessings all mine, with ten thousand beside!

Confused over your situation in life? Circumstances grinding away at you? Pressures too great to bear? Remember that friend's advice, "Just pray about it!" God showed gracious love to Judah, and He will do the same for you. Great is God's faithfulness! Seek Him in prayer. It may be that He will change your situation. But then again, it may be that He will change you! When Habakkuk prayed, God changed him. He was brought into conformity with God's will for his life.

Habakkuk 3:3-19

God came from Teman, and the Holy One from Mount Paran. Selah. His glory covered the heavens, and the earth was full of his praise. And his brightness was like the light; he had horns coming out of his hand; and there was the hiding of his power. Before him went the pestilence, and burning coals went forth at his feet. He stood, and measured the earth; he beheld, and drove asunder the nations; and the everlasting mountains were scattered, the perpetual hills did bow; his ways are everlasting. I saw the tents of Cushan in affliction: and the curtains of the land of Midian did tremble. Was the LORD displeased against the rivers? Was thine anger against the rivers? Was thy wrath against the sea, that thou didst ride upon thine horses and thy chariots of salvation? Thy bow was made quite naked, according to the oaths of the tribes, even thy word. Selah. Thou didst cleave the earth with rivers. The mountains saw thee, and they trembled; the overflowing of the water passed by; the deep uttered its voice, and lifted up its hands on high. The sun and moon stood still in their habitation; at the light of thine arrows they went, and at the shining of thy glittering spear. Thou didst march through the land in indignation; thou didst thresh the nations in anger. Thou wentest forth for the salvation of thy people, even for salvation with thine anointed; thou woundedst the head out of the house of the wicked, by laying bare the foundation unto the neck. Selah. Thou didst strike through with his own staves the head of his villages; they came out like a whirlwind to scatter me; their rejoicing was as if to devour the poor secretly. Thou didst walk through the sea with thine horses, through the heap of great waters. When I heard, my belly trembled, my lips quivered at the voice; rottenness entered into my bones, and I trembled in myself, that I might rest in the day of trouble. When he cometh up unto the people, he will invade them with his troops.

Although the fig tree shall not blossom, neither shall fruit be in the vines; the labor of the olive shall fail, and the fields shall yield no food; the flock shall be cut off from the fold, and there shall be no herd in the stalls; Yet I will rejoice in the LORD, I will joy in the God of my salvation. The LORD God is my strength, and he will make my feet like hinds' feet, and he will make me walk upon mine high places. To the chief singer on my stringed instruments.

PRAISING THE GOD WHO DELIVERS

Memory is a wonderful gift from God, but it can be a burden or a blessing. It was a burden when Habakkuk recalled the injustice taking place in Judah and God's seeming complacency to judge it. It was a burden when the prophet heard that God would use the savage Chaldeans to judge Judah. It was a burden as he patiently waited and watched for God's answer to his perplexity: *How can a holy God use a sinful nation to accomplish His righteous purpose?*

But memory was a blessing as well, especially when Habakkuk reflected on the lessons that he had learned from his experience. It was a blessing to hear that God would eventually destroy the Chaldeans and deliver His people from the tyrant's onslaught. It was a blessing to receive the revelation from God, "the just shall live by his faith." It was a blessing to remember that God is in control, and all things take place according to what He has purposed for His people. It was a blessing when he rejoiced over God's past deliverance and realized that it prefigured Israel's future deliverance. In celebration of its future deliverance, the prophet offered a hymn of praise as he portrayed, in poetic psalm, God's powerful deliverance of Israel throughout past centuries.

PORTRAIT OF GOD'S POWER

WONDERS IN THE SINAI

Habakkuk described God (Eloah) as the "Holy One" (v. 3), a name that expresses His absolute holiness and is in keeping with the spirit of this book (cp. 1:12-13).

His glory and power were mightily manifested to Israel when they were delivered from Egypt and received the Law at Mount Sinai. Habakkuk recalled this time when he said, "God came from Teman, and the Holy One from Mount Paran" (v. 3). Teman is in Edom, east of the Arabah, between the Dead Sea and the Gulf of Eilat. Paran is a mountainous desert area, west of Edom, in the Sinai Peninsula.

At this point, Habakkuk inserted "Selah" (v. 3), a musical notation whose meaning is uncertain. It is used in this chapter (vv. 3, 9, 13) as a pause to allow the reader time to reflect upon God's deliverance of His people.

First, God's glory "covered the heavens" (v. 3), evoking praise from the Israelites at Sinai. It streamed forth in great power: "And his brightness was like the light; he had horns [rays] coming out of his hand; and there was the hiding of his power" (v. 4). God's brilliant glory was inexplicable; it was like holding a candle to the sun in comparison. The phrase "horns coming out of his hand" (v. 4) is an anthropomorphic phrase (giving human form to God) to simply say that rays of God's glory were emitted in all directions. Although God's glory was greatly manifested, He still hid "his power" (v. 4) from the people, for no man can see God and live. So awesome was His glory that Moses had to be hidden in the "cleft of the rock" when God passed by (Ex. 33:18-23) or he would have perished.

God's glory was revealed at Mount Sinai as a "devouring fire on the top of the mount in the eyes of the children of Israel" (Ex. 24:17). God often has given glimpses of His glory. It was present in the holy of holies (Ex. 40:34); it filled Solomon's Temple (1 Ki. 8:10-11); the disciples saw it when Christ was transfigured before their eyes (Mt. 17:2); on the isle of Patmos, John saw the glorified Lord (Rev. 1:13-16). Today, believers can see the glory of God through Jesus Christ, for He is "the glory as of the only begotten of the Father, full of grace and truth" (Jn. 1:14). When the Lord returns to deliver Israel and set up the kingdom, "the earth shall be filled with the knowledge of the glory of the LORD, as the waters cover the sea" (2:14).

Second, Israel saw the power of the Lord. It was as "the pestilence, and burning coals [plague]" going "forth at his feet" (v. 5). When God passed through the earth to deliver Israel from Egypt, the land was full of pestilence and plague. The Israelites saw the same manifestation of God's power when they murmured in the wilderness. The glory and power revealed to Israel during that time will be experienced again when God destroys their enemies (v. 12) and delivers them in the future (v. 13).

WRATH ON SIN

God not only showed Israel the wonders of His glory and power, He also poured out wrath on their enemies. He is pictured as standing to measure the earth (v. 6) in preparation for judgment. Like a giant stepping off his land, God is pictured stepping off the area that

He will destroy. At His gaze, nations will be destroyed: "he beheld, and drove asunder the nations" (v. 6). The mountains and hills (v. 6), symbols of stability and permanence, although having been in existence since creation, will crumble at His gaze. Nothing will stand before God—neither nations nor nature.

There is a perpetuity with God. His "ways are everlasting" (v. 6). What He did for Israel in the past He can do in the future. God is immutable in His judgment of sin.

Two nations, Cushan and Midian (v. 7), were selected to illustrate how nations that opposed God and His people stood in fear.

Abruptly, Habakkuk shifted from speaking about God's judgment on nations to questioning Him concerning His wrath on nature: "Was the LORD displeased against the rivers?...Was thy wrath against the sea [Red Sea, Ex. 14:21-22; Jordan, Josh. 3:16], that thou didst ride upon thine horses [like a mighty warrior] and thy chariots of salvation [to physically deliver Israel from Egypt]?" (v. 8). No, God was not showing wrath against nature, but nature was affected when God brought physical deliverance to His people.

As a mighty warrior makes his "bow...quite naked" (v. 9)— that is, takes it from its case in preparation for battle—so God will defend His people "according to the oaths of the tribes" (v. 9). God will be true to His covenant promise to Israel. They (the oaths) never fail because they are based on His Word. Again, Habakkuk inserted a "Selah" (v. 9), pausing to reflect on God's promise.

The prophet reminded his readers that God did "cleave the earth with rivers" (v. 9). He may have had in mind the rivers at creation or those after the flood, but most likely he was referring to the dividing of the Red Sea when Israel was delivered from Egypt. In verse 10, the earth is personified—from the mountaintops to the depths of the sea—in order to express

God's great power and judgment. His power and judgment were clearly seen in the flood of Noah's day, but they will be seen in an even greater way during the Tribulation.

Habakkuk continued the imagery of God's power by referring to Joshua's long day, when he requested more light in order to defeat the Amorites at Gibeon (Josh. 10:12-14). At that time, "The sun and moon stood still in their habitation" (v. 11). "The light of thine arrows...and...the shining of thy glittering spear" (v. 11) express in poetic form the awesome lightning that shot forth from heaven and accompanied the storm that was sent on the Amorites. Habakkuk's point is evident: God exercises His mighty power in the form of miracles to deliver Israel.

WORK OF SALVATION

Having stood in awe at God's majesty and power, Habakkuk then focused on God's work of physical deliverance for Israel. In the past, God had marched "through the land in indignation" (v. 12), His purpose being to "thresh the nations" (v. 12) and bring "salvation" (physical deliverance, v. 13) to Israel. He acts with a purpose—never capriciously. If God has done this to Israel's enemies in the past, He will perform it in the future as well, when they are ripe for threshing.

When God delivers Judah, it will be through His "anointed" (v. 13). The phrase "with thine anointed" has been interpreted in many ways. Some scholars believe it refers to Israel as its own anointed deliverer, but the term is singular and is always used of a single person, not of a nation. Others hold that the reference is to a king, like David or Cyrus (Isa. 45:1) the Persian (558-529 B.C.), who would deliver Judah from the Babylonian captivity (Isa. 44:28). Still others believe the phrase refers to the Messiah who was and will be the agent of Israel's deliverance.[1] Most likely the reference is to Cyrus, who was the anointed representative and delivered Israel from Babylon.

Israel would be delivered by God's anointed, who "woundedst [crushed] the head out of [from] the house of the wicked [one], by laying bare the foundation unto the neck" (v. 13). This is an allegorical picture of Babylon's impregnable walls being torn down from top to bottom (Jer. 51).

Upon reading this prophecy, Judah would recall God's great deliverance of their forefathers from Egypt and take hope, being certain that God would deliver them from the Chaldeans.

This is a picture of Israel's final deliverance, when Jesus (God's Anointed) will crush Gentile world rule (Dan. 2:44-45) and destroy the armies of the world at Armageddon (Rev. 19:19-21). Once again, a crescendo of this poetic prophecy is reached with the word "Selah" (v. 13).

Habakkuk went on to describe what would happen to his enemies. They would destroy themselves: "Thou didst strike through with his own staves [shafts] the head of his villages" (v. 14). The enemies of Israel would be brought to confusion and actually fight among themselves. This happened a number of times in Israel's history. It happened when the Midianites destroyed themselves in the days of Gideon (Jud. 7:22). It happened when God delivered the Philistines to Jonathan (1 Sam. 14:16, 20) and when Ammon, Moab, and Edom fought among themselves (2 Chr. 20:22-23). It will happen again when Russia descends upon the mountains of Israel (Ezek. 38:21). In the case of Babylon, the Medes joined them to destroy the Assyrians, but then the Medes turned on Babylon to destroy them (Jer. 51:11, 28).

Before the Babylonians were destroyed, they came on Judah like a "whirlwind to scatter" them (v. 14). So fierce were the Babylonians that they descended like a tornado that blows everything away. They rejoiced with devilish pleasure at their victories, as would thieves and murderers who secretly wait to rob and kill defenseless travelers. The "poor" (v. 14) were unprotected Judeans who were at the mercy of the Babylonians as they hunted unprotected people to rob and murder.

But the Babylonians' rejoicing was premature. Using a figure from the Red Sea deliverance, Habakkuk portrayed God as a mighty warrior riding His chariot through the sea to destroy Israel's enemies and bring about deliverance. Nothing stands in the way of God to deliver His people! What great encouragement this was to Habakkuk. By recalling past deliverances, Judah could be assured of future liberation from their enemies. The Lord will ride out of the clouds of heaven to deliver Israel from the armies of the world at Armageddon (Rev. 19:11).

PONDERING GOD'S POWER

In the final section of Habakkuk's poetic psalm, the tempo changed from excitement to a spirit of calm assurance concerning Judah's victory over their enemies. As stated in verse 2, Habakkuk knew that judgment was inevitable, and this struck terror in his heart.

FEARING GOD'S POWER

Upon hearing about God's judgment, Habakkuk said, "my belly [inner being] trembled, my lips quivered at the voice [the judgment left him speechless]; rottenness entered my bones [his body became weak with fear], and I trembled in myself [it was like he reeled back and forth on the spot where he stood]" (v. 16).

Yet, the knowledge of God's future deliverance filled Habakkuk with trust. He could say, "I might rest in the day of trouble. When he cometh up unto the people, he will invade them with his troops" (v. 16).

What beautiful confidence in God! Although shocked by the initial news of judgment upon Judah, Habakkuk had perfect peace in the midst of the terror all around him.

FAITH IN GOD'S PURPOSE

The devastation left by Babylon would be awesome (see Lamentations). Judah would be depleted of all its natural resources: "the fig tree shall not blossom, neither shall fruit be in the vines; the labor of the olive shall fail, and the fields shall yield no food; the flock shall be cut off from the fold, and there shall be no herd in the stalls" (v. 17). In modern times, we might say, *Although the bank account is depleted, the refrigerator is empty, and the heater is broken....*

In spite of it all, Habakkuk could say, "Yet I will rejoice in the LORD. I will joy in the God of my salvation" (v. 18). He stood firm, unshaken, as a testimony to the faithful in Judah. He looked beyond the impending judgment to the time of salvation (deliverance). Habakkuk's eyes were not focused on his circumstances but on God.

The prophet's faith reached its peak with the expression, "The LORD God is my strength" (v. 19). The strength Habakkuk felt from the Lord is illustrated by the hind. The deer is weak to protect itself from predators, but when it sniffs danger, its strong hind legs spring into action and carry it swiftly to the mountain summit, where safety awaits. The deer is able to walk with security on the steep and slippery sides of the summit without fear of savage beasts snuffing out its life. When David was delivered from the hands of Saul, he expressed his gratitude to the Lord with the same words: "He maketh my feet like hinds' feet, and setteth me upon my high places" (2 Sam. 22:34; Ps. 18:33).

Like the deer, Habakkuk was able to "walk upon...high places" (v. 19), an expression used to denote that he was living victoriously over his circumstances.

Habakkuk had come full circle. He had triumphed over doubt, discouragement, despair, and defeat. He began in the valley asking, *Why Lord?* He was lifted by a vision: "the just shall live by his faith." Finally, he walked victoriously, lived above his circumstances, and rejoiced in the God of his salvation.

Like the prophet, you may have *Why?* questions that God has not chosen to answer as yet. And like him, you must not become weary in waiting and watching for the answers. God is working, for "we know that all things work together for good to them that love God, to them who are the called according to his purpose" (Rom. 8:28). The key to victory is to walk in worship, knowing that God will answer in His own time and in His own way. Although Habakkuk had not personally experienced God's deliverance, he was able to say, "I will joy in the God of my salvation." Why not do the same?

ENDNOTES

CHAPTER 1

[1] Abigail Van Buren, *Family Helps, There's No Such Thing as an Average Day in America* (Chattanooga: AMG International), vol. 2, num. 7, p. 6.

[2] Jim Larson, *Family Life, Today's Family: Essential or Expendable?* (Los Angeles: The American Institute of Family Relations, September and October 1978).

[3] *Family Helps, Teenagers and Premarital Sex* (Chattanooga: AMG International), vol. 3, num. 10, p. 1.

[4] *Ibid.*, p. 4.

[5] *Family Helps, The Influence of TV* (Chattanooga: AMG International), vol. 3, num. 12, p. 2.

[6] *Family Helps, TV Watching and Intelligence* (Chattanooga: AMG International), vol. 3, num. 10, p. 6.

CHAPTER 2

[1] Frederick A. Tatford, *The Minor Prophets: Prophet of the Watchtower: An Exposition of Habakkuk* (Minneapolis: Klock and Klock Christian Publishers, Inc., 1982), vol. II, p. 24.

CHAPTER 3

[1] Arthur W. Pink, *The Attributes of God* (Grand Rapids: Baker Book House, 1975), p. 52.

[2] Oswald Chambers, *My Utmost for His Highest* (New York: Dodd, Mead, and Company, 1956), p. 285.

[3] *Ibid.*

CHAPTER 4

[1] V. Raymond Edman, *The Disciplines of Life* (Wheaton: Van Kampen Press, 1948), p. 79.

[2] *Ibid.*, pp. 80-81.

[3] *Ibid.*, p. 82.

CHAPTER 5

[1] Merrill F. Unger, *Unger's Commentary on the Old Testament: Habakkuk* (Chicago: Moody Press, 1981), vol. II, p. 1905.

[2] H. L. Wilmington, *Wilmington's Guide to the Bible* (Wheaton: Tyndale House Publishers, Inc., 1981), pp. 231-32.

[3] Spiros Zodhiates, *Pulpit Helps, N.E.W.S. of Significance* (Chattanooga: AMB Publishers), a number of quotations taken from various issues.

CHAPTER 6

[1] Merrill F. Unger, *Unger's Commentary on the Old Testament* (Chicago: Moody Press, 1981), vol. II, p. 1910.

[2] C. Laird Harris, Gleason L. Archer, Jr., Bruce K. Waltke, *Theological Wordbook of the Old Testament* (Chicago: Moody Press, 1980), vol. II, pp. 841-42.

[3] Walter C. Kaiser, Jr., *A Biblical Approach to Personal Suffering* (Chicago: Moody Press, 1982), p. 79.

CHAPTER 7

[1] It is interesting to note that the term "anointed" (v. 13) is *Messiah* in Hebrew and *Christ* in Greek. The word for "salvation" (v. 13), which is used twice in this verse, is from the Hebrew word *Yeshua*, which is the same as *Jesus* in Greek.

RECOMMENDED READING

Barber, Cyril J. *Everyman's Bible Commentary: Habakkuk and Zephaniah.* Chicago: Moody Press, 1985.

Blue, J. Ronald. *The Bible Knowledge Commentary: Habakkuk.* Wheaton: Victor Books, 1985.

Bullock, C. Hassell. *An Introduction to the Old Testament Prophetic Books.* Chicago: Moody Press, 1986.

Feinberg, Charles L. *The Minor Prophets.* Chicago: Moody Press, 1961.

Freeman, Hobart E. *An Introduction to the Old Testament Prophets.* Chicago: Moody Press, 1968.

_____. *Everyman's Bible Commentary: Nahum, Zephaniah, Habakkuk: Minor Prophets of the Seventh Century B.C.* Chicago: Moody Press, 1973.

Gaebelein, Frank E. *Four Minor Prophets: Obadiah, Jonah, Habakkuk, and Haggai.* Chicago: Moody Press, 1977.

Ironside, H. A. *Notes on the Minor Prophets.* Neptune, NJ: Loizeaux Brothers, 1909.

Kaiser, Walter C., Jr. *A Biblical Approach to Personal Suffering.* Chicago: Moody Press, 1982.

Keil, C. F. *Biblical Commentary on the Old Testament: Minor Prophets: Habakkuk,* vol. 2. Grand Rapids: Wm. B. Eerdmans, 1949.

Lloyd-Jones, D. Martin. *From Fear to Faith.* Grand Rapids: Baker Book House, 1982.

Pusey, E. B. *The Minor Prophets: A Commentary,* vol. 2. Grand Rapids: Baker Book House, 1950.

Tatford, Frederick A. *The Minor Prophets: Prophet of the Watchtower: An Exposition of Habakkuk,* vol. 2. Minneapolis: Klock and Klock Christian Publishers, Inc., 1982.

Unger, Merrill F. *Unger's Commentary on the Old Testament: Habakkuk,* vol. 2. Chicago: Moody Press, 1981.

Wiersbe, Warren W. *From Worry to Worship: Studies in Habakkuk.* Lincoln, NE: Back to the Bible, 1983.

PART II
ZEPHANIAH

INTRODUCTION

Zephaniah's name means *Jehovah hides* or *Jehovah protects.* For this reason, some scholars have conjectured that he was born in the latter part of Manasseh's reign (686-642 B.C.; cp. 2 Ki. 21:16). He had social standing in the courts of Judah, being the great-great-grandson of King Hezekiah (1:1). He ministered during the reign of King Josiah, a godly ruler and a relative of the prophet. Although his hometown is not mentioned, he probably lived in or near Jerusalem. The prophet's occupation is unknown. Zephaniah dated his prophecy during Josiah's reign (640-609 B.C.), and he was a contemporary of Jeremiah, Nahum, and Habakkuk. Because Zephaniah did not mention the reforms of Josiah, which took place in the 18th year of the king's reign (2 Chr. 34:8), he must have written before 622 B.C.

The background for Zephaniah's prophecy was a time of social, moral, and religious decay (3:1-7). Hezekiah was succeeded by his son Manasseh (695-642 B.C.), who reigned for 55 years. He was the most wicked king in Judah's history. He revived Baal worship, made his son pass through the fire, observed times, used enchantments, and dealt with mediums and wizards (2 Ki. 21; 2 Chr. 33:1-9). After being taken captive to Babylon and later released, he tried to reverse his wickedness, but without success (2 Chr. 33:10-20). Amon (642-640 B.C.), Manasseh's son, took the throne after his father's death and continued the idolatry of his father. He was assassinated by his servants only two years into his reign (2 Chr. 33:21-25).

Amon was succeeded by his son Josiah (640-609 B.C.), who was only eight years old at the time. At the age of 16, Josiah began to seek the Lord (2 Chr. 34:3). It was at that time, while repairing the Temple, that Hilkiah the high priest found the book of the law and read it to Josiah. After reading the law, Josiah instituted many moral and religious reforms (2 Ki. 23). Following the Temple's cleansing, a great Passover was held (2 Ki. 22-23; 2 Chr. 34-35).

At the beginning of Josiah's reign, Judah was subservient to Assyria, who held political supremacy over the nations in the Middle East. Upon the death of Ashurbanipal (633 B.C.), the Syrian Empire started to decline. During that time, the Medes and Babylonians (612 B.C.) conquered the Assyrians. Ashur-uballit (612-608 B.C.) fled from Assyria to Haran and established his court in exile. Pharaoh-neco of Egypt came north (609 B.C.) to help Ashur-uballit, and Josiah tried to stop him at Megiddo. Although successful in stopping Egypt from helping Ashur-uballit of Assyria, Josiah was killed in the battle (2 Chr. 35:20-25).

Four years later, Nebuchadnezzar defeated Pharaoh-neco at Carchemish. Judah tried to help the Babylonians by fighting Egypt, but in the process they lost their king and became a vassal to the nation they tried to assist. Later, the Babylonians totally destroyed Judah (586 B.C.).

The purpose of Zephaniah's prophecy was to announce the coming Day of the Lord, or judgment on Judah. Zephaniah ended his prophecy with a note of hope. When the Messiah returns to the earth, He will gather Israel back to its land and provide redemption and restoration to the nation.

Some of the key words in Zephaniah are *Day of the Lord, that day, desolation,* and *remnant.* There are two key verses in the book: "Hold thy peace at the presence of the Lord GOD; for the day of the LORD is at hand; for the LORD hath prepared a sacrifice, he hath bidden his guests" (1:7) and "The LORD hath taken away thy judgments, he hath cast out thine enemy; the King of Israel, even the LORD, is in the midst of thee, thou shalt not see evil any more" (3:15).

Zephaniah 1:1-6

The word of the LORD which came unto Zephaniah, the son of Cushi, the son of Gedaliah, the son of Amariah, the son of Hezekiah, in the days of Josiah, the son of Amon, king of Judah. I will utterly consume all things from off the land, saith the LORD. I will consume man and beast; I will consume the fowls of the heavens, and the fish of the sea, and the stumbling blocks with the wicked; and I will cut off man from the land, saith the LORD. I will also stretch out mine hand upon Judah, and upon all the inhabitants of Jerusalem; and I will cut off the remnant of Baal from this place, and the name of the Chemarim with the priests; And those who worship the host of heaven upon the housetops; and those who worship and who swear by the LORD, and who swear by Malcam; And those who are turned back from the LORD; and those who have not sought the LORD, nor inquired for him.

WARNING THE WICKED

The 1990s will go down in history as a decade of unprecedented changes worldwide. Eastern Europe is swiftly evolving into a Western-style society. Europe will be sporting a new look known as the European Economic Community in the not-too-distant future. The unification of Germany, unthinkable a few years ago, is symbolic of rapid change and a new day coming in Europe. World leaders are hoping that these international changes will precipitate global peace by the 21st century.

Similar political changes were taking place in Zephaniah's day. New coalitions were being formed between nations in the East. Assyria and Egypt had become allies, as had the Medes and Babylonians. Assyria was on the decline as a superpower, and a Neo-Babylonian Empire was on the rise. There was a power vacuum in the East, allowing smaller nations like Judah to prosper politically and expand their military influence beyond national boundaries.[1]

Judah and neighboring nations desired such peace, power, and prosperity, but it was not to be. An obscure prophet named Zephaniah stepped onto the stage of history and announced that judgment, not peace, was soon to come—a time the prophet would later call "the day of the LORD."

WORD TO JUDAH

Zephaniah's mission was to convey "The word of the LORD" (v. 1) to Judah, a word of unparalleled tribulation and destruction that the nations of the world and the people of Judah were to experience.

Zephaniah did not come from a common background. He had an aristocratic lineage and traced his pedigree through four generations of kings: "the son of Cushi…Gedaliah…Amariah…Hezekiah" (v. 1), thus making him the great-great-grandson of King Hezekiah. By mentioning his genealogy, Zephaniah distinguished himself from three other men who bore the same name (2 Ki. 25:18-21; 1 Chr. 6:36-38; Zech. 6:10, 14). It gave him credibility as a reformer like Hezekiah—who abolished idolatry from Judah—and revealed that he was a relative of King Josiah (640-609 B.C.), in whose reign he prophesied (v. 1).

Scholars are divided on whether Zephaniah prophesied before or after the religious reforms of King Josiah. Internal evidence seems to suggest that he prophesied just before those reforms, which occurred in 622 B.C.

WRATH OF JEHOVAH

Before launching into his message on Judah's judgment, Zephaniah revealed that God is the judge of the earth, thereby establishing the power and scope of God's judgment. Ultimately, the Lord "will utterly consume all things from off the land" (v. 2). All life associated with the earth will be destroyed—man, beasts, fowls, and the fish of the sea (v. 3). Interestingly, the prophet described the various forms of life to be destroyed in the reverse order of their creation. Zephaniah went on to say that when judgment came, God would destroy "the stumbling blocks [ruins] with the wicked" (v. 3). This phrase could be interpreted in one of two ways. Some scholars believe that the earth will be in ruin or rubble when God removes the wicked from it. Others hold that "stumbling blocks" are those religious rites and objects used in idolatrous worship, and God will remove them with the wicked at the time of judgment. The latter view best fits the context.

God reemphasized, "I will cut off man from the land" (v. 3). There is an interesting word play between *man* (Heb., *adam*) and *land* (Heb., *adamah*). Man—who was created from the land, whose life was sustained by it, and who brought about its curse through his sin—will be removed from the land by God's universal judgment.[2] The certainty of this judgment is confirmed by the words "saith the LORD" (v. 3).

The ultimate fulfillment of this judgment will take place at the end of the Great Tribulation, when the earth will be almost totally entrenched in idolatry. During that time, the world will worship the Antichrist and his image as God. Although God will bring universal judgment upon the wicked during that period, He will spare a righteous remnant (Zeph. 3:9-13) from being consumed.

The word *consume* is used three times in verses 2 and 3, presenting a picture of a person sweeping a building clean, bundling up the worthless items, and hauling away the debris to be buried or burned.

Peter revealed that during the Day of the Lord, "the heavens shall pass away with a great noise, and the elements shall melt with fervent heat; the earth also, and the works that are in it, shall be burned up" (2 Pet. 3:10). Ultimately, the Lord will dissolve the physical elements of the earth, along with all its sinful deeds. The atoms, neutrons, protons, and electrons, in their present form, will be consumed by fire. The word *heavens* speaks of the physical universe. It will pass away with a "great noise"—that is, a loud crackling or whistling sound as the elements of the physical earth and universe are consumed by the hand of Almighty God. In its place will appear the "new heavens and a new earth, in which dwelleth righteousness" (2 Pet. 3:13).

WICKEDNESS OF JUDAH

Zephaniah abruptly switched the emphasis of his prophecy from worldwide judgment to the coming punishment of Judah. God said, "I will also stretch out mine hand upon Judah, and upon all the inhabitants of Jerusalem" (v. 4). Judah had felt the blessing of God's "mighty hand, and…outstretched arm" (Dt. 26:8; cp. Ex. 6:6) when He delivered them from the Egyptians. But now God's privileged people, because of their wickedness, would be destroyed by His hand (Jer. 21:5-7).

The prophet named five types of wickedness for which Judah would be judged. First, they were guilty of the *sacrilegious* worship of Baal (v. 4). The name *Baal* means *master* or *lord* and is often used synonymously with idolatry. Describing the vile worship of Baalism, Dr. Barber wrote,

> In the Canaanite pantheon, Baal was the son of El. He was the god of fertility as well as the god of the storm and of war. His worship was extremely sensual. Open immorality was practiced "on every high hill" and "under every green tree" (1 Ki. 14:23). Baal's sister-consort was Anat, sometimes referred to as Anath. Her characteristic complemented his.

Religious or "sacred" prostitution was practiced in her name by the priestesses connected with her temples. All of that was done to ensure the fertility of the earth and an abundant harvest. It was believed that if Baal and Anat saw humans cohabiting on the earth, they would be reminded of their own conjugal responsibilities. Their cosmic union would then produce on earth bountiful crops and increase the size of flocks and herds.[3]

God strongly condemned these abominable practices. His law clearly taught that the land itself would vomit out the Canaanites (Lev. 18:25) for such practices, and if Israel did not heed God's warning, the land would spew it out as well (Lev. 18:28).

Zephaniah foretold that God would also "cut off...the name of the Chemarim with the priests" (v. 4). The name *Chemarim* (*idol-priests*) refers to foreign priests brought into Judah to conduct Baal worship. Zephaniah also prophesied that no form of Baal worship would remain in Judah after God's judgment. Although King Josiah tried to rid the land of idolatry (2 Ki. 23:4-24), it later reappeared. The Babylonian captivity eventually did rid Israel of idol worship forever.

Second, there were those in Judah who practiced *Sabaism* by bowing down to "the host of heaven upon the housetops" (v. 5). They erected family altars on the flat roofs of their homes and burned incense in the morning and evening to the sun, moon, and stars (Jer. 19:13; 32:29).

Judah was also guilty of worshiping the "queen of heaven" (Jer. 7:18; 44:17, 19, 25), who was probably the goddess Ashtoreth (equivalent to the Babylonian-Assyrian goddess Ishtar, the Canaanite Astarte, the Greek Aphrodite, and the Roman Venus). She was the goddess of sensual love, maternity, and fertility. Licentious worship was conducted in her honor. The great King

Solomon erected idols to this goddess in Jerusalem (1 Ki. 11:5), and the wicked King Manasseh reestablished worship to her years later (2 Ki. 23:13). In Scripture, she is called Ashtoreth instead of Ashtaroth, her ancient name. The writers of Scripture altered her name, giving it the vowels of their word for *shame*.[4]

The law condemned such practices (Dt. 16:21-22; 17:2-5; 2 Ki. 17:16). The sin of stellar worship contributed heavily to the collapse and ultimate destruction of the ten tribes of Israel. With such knowledge at hand, it is reasonable to assume that Judah's kings would not have become involved in Sabaism, but such was not the case.

Of those Americans who are involved in astrology, most deny that they worship the stars; however, many practice horoscope reading and gear their day according to its predictions. This holds true for many evangelical Christians as well. A Gallup poll indicates that the stars influence people's lives, and many Christians consult their daily or weekly horoscopes. The poll also revealed that among teenagers (ages 13-18), 55 percent believe in astrology. Ten percent of evangelicals believe in astrology. More than 80 percent of all United States newspapers now carry horoscope columns. Astrology is estimated to be anywhere from a $200 million to a $1 billion-a-year industry. A CNN report cited astrologers who claim that "at least 300 of the Fortune 500 [companies] use astrologers in one way or another."[5]

Gallup, Roper, and Greeley polls have indicated that tens of millions of people are involved in the occult. The University of Chicago national opinion poll revealed that 67 percent of Americans believe in the supernatural and that 42 percent believe that they have been in contact with someone who has died. Profits from channeled (spirit-originated) seminars, tapes, and books alone range from $100 to $500 million a year. The late Dr. Walter Martin estimated that more than 100 million Americans were actively or peripherally involved in occult practices.[6] "According to Marilyn

McGuire, Executive Director of the New Age Publishing and Retailing Alliance, there are some 2,500 occult bookstores in the U.S. and over 3,000 publishers of occult books and journals."[7] If God judged other nations for trusting in the stars for divine guidance, He may also judge our nation for the same sin.

Third, the Judeans were guilty of *syncretistic* worship, for they swore to the Lord as well as to Malcam (v. 5). The Judeans were binding themselves to God by an oath, while at the same time calling upon Malcam as god.

The name *Malcam* is synonymous with Molech (Lev. 18:21) and Milcom (1 Ki. 11:5), the national god of the Ammonites. They believed him to be a protecting father and honored him by sacrificing their children to him (Jer. 32:35). Although the worship of Molech was forbidden in the law (Lev. 18:21; 20:1-5), Solomon built an altar to him at Topheth in the Valley of Hinnom, and Manasseh honored him through idolatrous orgies and the sacrifice of his own son (2 Ki. 21:6). King Josiah desecrated the altar in the Hinnom Valley (2 Ki. 23:10), but Jehoiakim later revived the cult (2 Ki. 23:37).[8]

Although such evil types of worship are not practiced today (with the exception of Satanism), many people are syncretistic in their beliefs. Some people who claim to be Christians are involved in organizations that embrace ancient religious systems condemned in the Bible.

A modern-day form of syncretistic belief is practiced in the Masonic Lodge, a fact that has recently come to light through the research of John Ankerberg and John Weldon. They wrote,

> The Masonic Lodge teaches in the Royal Arch degree that it knows the true name of God. The candidate is instructed that from now on the true name of God is Jahbulon....The term Jahbulon is a composite term for Jehovah (Jah), Baal

(Bul or Bel), and Osiris (On, a corruption of Os). Masonic authorities such as Coil and *The Masonic Ritual* admit that "Bul" or "Bel" refers to the Assyrian or Canaanite deity Baal and that "On" refers to the Egyptian deity Osiris. Wagner reveals the Masonic goal in this pagan trinity: In this compound name an attempt is made to show by a coordination of divine names…the unity, identity and harmony of the Hebrew, Assyrian and Egyptian god-ideas, and the harmony of the Royal Arch religion with these ancient religions. This Masonic "unity of God" is peculiar. It is the doctrine that the different names of gods [such as] Brahma, Jehovah, Baal, Bel, Om, On, etc., all denote the generative procreative principle, in that all religions are essentially the same in their ideas of the divine.[9]

Masons would not think of incorporating Baal worship into their beliefs or practices, but they follow a syncretistic-type teaching by combining these gods with the true God of the Bible. Such practices are condemned by God.

Fourth, there was a group within Judah who *separated* from God. They were "those who are turned back from the LORD" (v. 6). These people knew the law and had at one time worshiped God, but eventually they became apostates. The word *apostasy* means *a falling away*—a deliberate and total abandonment of the faith previously professed but not possessed. Such a falling away was evident in Zephaniah's description of Judah's religious practices.

Apparently apostate teachings are finding fertile ground in which to germinate through some churches and seminaries today. A report in *Redbook* magazine revealed that in a survey of ministers in training, "56% rejected the virgin birth, 71% rejected life after death, 54% rejected the bodily resurrection of Jesus Christ, and 98% rejected Christ's return to earth."[10]

Fifth, there were *secularists,* "those who have not sought the LORD, nor inquired for him" (v. 6). Although this group was not involved in evil worship, they were indifferent to religion altogether. The same could be said of many Israelis today. About 45 percent are secular Jews and do not practice their religion. In the United States, the number is even higher—at least 55 percent of the Jewish population is not affiliated with a synagogue. An even higher percentage of Gentiles in America is secularist and does not practice any religion.

Yet there seems to be a new trend emerging in America. Many secularists, longing for meaning to their existence, have turned to religious experience. All too often, however, they become entangled in the popular religious fads of the day—cults or the occult—which ultimately leave them unfulfilled. The most popular religious fad today is the New Age movement, which is steeped in Eastern philosophical religious mysticism.

Within 50 years of Zephaniah's prediction, judgment fell on Judah. Its judgment was total, its captivity complete; nothing went untouched when the Day of the Lord came.

Zephaniah's prophecy is a mirror of the spiritual and moral declension we sense taking place in America. Could it be that the Day of the Lord is about to appear on the horizon of this country?

Zephaniah 1:7-2:3

Hold thy peace at the presence of the Lord GOD; for the day of the LORD is at hand; for the LORD hath prepared a sacrifice, he hath bidden his guests. And it shall come to pass in the day of the LORD's sacrifice, that I will punish the princes, and the king's children, and all such as are clothed with foreign apparel. In the same day also will I punish all those who leap on the threshold, who fill their masters' houses with violence and deceit. And it shall come to pass in that day, saith the LORD, that there shall be the noise of a cry from the fish gate, and a wailing from the second quarter, and a great crashing from the hills. Wail, ye inhabitants of Maktesh; for all the merchant people are cut down, all they that bear silver are cut off. And it shall come to pass at that time, that I will search Jerusalem with lamps, and punish the men that are settled on their lees, that say in their heart, The LORD will not do good, neither will he do evil. Therefore, their goods shall become a booty, and their houses a desolation; they shall also build houses, but not inhabit them; and they shall plant vineyards, but not drink the wine of them. The great day of the LORD is near, it is near, and hasteneth greatly, even the voice of the day of the LORD; the mighty man shall cry there bitterly. That day is a day of wrath, a day of trouble and distress, a day of waste and desolation, a day of darkness and gloominess, a day of clouds and thick darkness, A day of the trumpet and alarm against the fortified cities, and against the high towers. And I will bring distress upon men, that they shall walk like blind men, because they have sinned against the LORD; and their blood shall be poured out like dust, and their flesh like the dung. Neither their silver nor their gold shall be able to deliver them in the day of the LORD's wrath, but the whole land shall be devoured by the fire of his jealousy; for he shall make even a speedy riddance of all those who dwell in the land.

Gather yourselves together, yea, gather together, O nation not desired, Before the decree bring forth, before the day pass like the chaff, before the fierce anger of the LORD come upon you, before the day of the LORD's anger come upon you. Seek the LORD, all ye meek of the earth, who have kept his ordinances; seek righteousness, seek meekness; it may be ye shall be hidden in the day of the LORD's anger.

THE DAY OF THE LORD

On June 22, 1990, a massive earthquake rocked northern Iran just after midnight. Iranian radio estimated the death toll to be approximately 45,000, with as many as 130,000 injured. Entire villages were either reduced to rubble or completely buried in less than one minute. Most North Americans are unable to comprehend that kind of devastation, never having experienced an earthquake of such magnitude.

In the July 2, 1990, issue of *Time* magazine, it was called "The Hour of Doom." *Newsweek*, in their July 2, 1990, issue, called it "Enduring a Test of God." Little did these bureau reporters know the prophetic overtones of their captions. A day is coming when such devastation will sweep the entire earth—a day called, in biblical terms, the Day of the Lord.

NEED FOR JUDGMENT

Zephaniah announced that God was prepared to judge Judah. He went on to say, "Hold thy peace at the presence of the Lord GOD; for the day of the LORD is at hand" (v. 7). The people were to remain silent before the sovereign Lord of the universe. Pleading for mercy would not turn away His vengeance, for God's judgment was ready to fall on the nation.

The judgment is described as "a [His] sacrifice" for which God had already "bidden [appointed] his guests" (v. 7). Judah was to be the sacrifice, and the hated Babylonians were the guests who would slaughter the nation and devour it, like an animal sacrificed in the Temple.

Zephaniah mentioned seven groups who would suffer the judgment of God. First, the "princes" (v. 8)—those serving as judges, magistrates, and aristocrats in the king's court—would be judged. These leaders should have been prime examples of morality, righteousness, and justice in the nation, but instead they were the main promoters of wickedness, severely oppressing the people.

Second, the king's posterity would suffer judgment. After Josiah's death, God would not allow his children (v. 8) to have long or successful reigns. Jehoahaz's rule lasted only three months (2 Ki. 23:31-34). King Jehoiakim ruled for 11 years (2 Ki. 23:36) but was defeated by Nebuchadnezzar (2 Ki. 24:1-2). Jehoiachin's reign lasted only three months before he was deported to Babylon (2 Ki. 24:8-16). Judah's last king, Zedekiah, ruled for 11 years but was eventually taken captive, blinded, and deported to Babylon (2 Ki. 24:18-25:7).

The iron-fisted rule of despots in Eastern Europe is a prime example of such oppression in this century. These Communist leaders committed unbelievable atrocities against their people, milking their countries of their resources while they themselves lived in luxury. Judgment has fallen on many of them. In the wake of socialistic reforms, some of these leaders have been removed from office in disgrace, some have been imprisoned, and others have been executed.

The rebellion of Judah's leaders was seen in their dress: "such as are clothed with foreign apparel" (v. 8). Adopting such outward dress meant that the leaders had assumed the customs, habits, and manners of their godless neighbors—Egypt, Assyria, and Babylon. They took on the look of worldly materialism. Isaiah put it well when he said, "The show of their countenance doth witness against them" (Isa. 3:9).

The Lord had set forth certain requirements regarding clothing for the Israelites (Dt. 22:11-12). The reason for not mixing wool and linen in the same garment is uncertain. It may have been a pagan practice from which Israel was being protected. The Israelites were commanded to put fringes (tassels) on their garments to serve as a reminder of the Lord's commandments and their covenant commitment to obey them (Num. 15:37-40). In like manner, Peter reminded Christian women that their clothing is to be consistent with godliness (1 Pet. 3:3-4). Such is not the case with many Christian men and women today, who dress in a worldly manner.

Third, the plunderers would be judged, "those who leap on [over] the threshold, who fill their masters' houses with violence and deceit" (v. 9). The term *leap on the threshold* may refer to the Philistines' superstitious practice of not stepping on a threshold because the image of their god Dagon had fallen on the threshold in his pagan temple (1 Sam. 5:4-5), or a quick entrance into someone else's house for the purpose of robbery. The latter view seems more likely. Such base people were retained by their masters (political leaders in the king's court) to acquire wealth by violent and fraudulent means.

Fourth, people in every area of Jerusalem—the "fish gate [northern section]…the second quarter [new city, northwest of the Temple], and…from the hills [the whole area of the city]" (v. 10)—would wail in agony when God's judgment fell. There would be howling and shrieking, intermingled with the triumphant shouts of the enemy as they plundered and slew the people. In the background would be heard the crash of houses, palaces, and the Temple as they were being destroyed.

Fifth, the polluted business district would be destroyed. "For all the merchant people are cut down, all they that bear silver are cut off" (v. 11). They were located in the "Maktesh" (a mortar or hollow, v. 11), the lower section running north and south along the Temple wall known as the Tyropean Valley. In this market area, Jewish merchants and money changers conducted their business.

Zephaniah called them "merchant people" (v. 11), a contemptuous phrase meaning *people of Canaan* and used of the unscrupulous Phoenicians who were shrewd, greedy, and dishonest in trading and usury. Apparently the Jewish merchants had become like the Canaanites in the way they conducted their business. Both the merchants and the money changers (those laden with silver) would be cut off.

Sixth, the passionless people of Jerusalem—"the men that are settled on their lees" (v. 12)—would be destroyed. The *lees* are *dregs* that must be separated from wine during its processing. If the dregs are left in the wine too long, it becomes a thick, bitter syrup. Thus, to settle on the lees is to become hardened, spiritually complacent, and callous in character and conduct. Instead of cleansing themselves of the dregs of sin through daily repentance, the people of Judah had settled into the dregs of impurity, practicing the moral wickedness of their heathen neighbors.[1] Then they projected their own spiritual impurity and complacency upon the Lord by saying, "The LORD will not do good, neither will he do evil" (v. 12). They had become so indifferent to God that they viewed Him in the same light as a pagan idol, having neither interest in nor the ability to intervene in the affairs of mankind. They had come to the point of denying God's divine providence in the universe, as well as His power and promise to deliver from divine judgment.[2]

This is true today of some in the church who profess to be Christians. They consider God to be their Savior but not their sovereign Lord. They give Him lip service from time to time, but they live as if God cares little about them personally and has no control over the circumstances of their lives.

The Lord will "search Jerusalem with lamps" (v. 12), seeking such people to judge. God is pictured as diligently searching every area of Jerusalem, just as a person searches every corner of a darkened room. During the Roman destruction of Jerusalem in 70 A.D., the inhabitants of the city were dragged out of sewers, holes, caves, and tombs to be put to death.[3] Of course, we cannot forget that God uses the same diligence to seek and to save those who are lost (Lk. 15:8-10).

Seventh, the property of the wealthy would be destroyed: "their goods shall become a booty, and their houses a desolation" (v. 13). God would not allow them to enjoy the houses and vineyards they had obtained through ill-gotten gain. God would prove to Judah that He keeps His promises by stripping such wealthy people of their possessions.

Paul warned that Christians who seek riches fall into temptations, traps, and dangerous desires that can plunge them into ruin and destruction. In fact, those who are eager to gain wealth have actually wandered from the faith and pierced themselves with many sorrows. Paul admonished believers to flee from seeking wealth and to pursue righteousness and godliness (1 Tim. 6:9-11). This is a message that every believer should heed in this age of materialism.

NEARNESS OF JUDGMENT

Once again Zephaniah returned to his theme, this time emphasizing twice the nearness of "The great day of the LORD" (v. 14). He underscored its imminence by stating that "it is near, and hasteneth greatly [speedily]" toward its coming (v. 14). The word *near* is in the emphatic position to stress how quickly it will come. It is so close that the voice (sound) of its coming can be heard (v. 14).

How true were the prophet's words. It was near for the Assyrians, who were destroyed in 612 B.C. It was near for Judah, who suffered three waves of Babylonian persecution and was finally destroyed in 586 B.C. It was near for the Babylonians, who were destroyed by the Medo-Persian Empire in 539 B.C.

The future Day of the Lord will be so awesome in its terror that "the mighty man shall cry there bitterly" (v. 14). Even battle-hardened warriors, fearing neither conflict nor man, will cry in terror like frightened children when the Lord's judgment comes. This awesome day of God's wrath will be a time of total destruction. A vivid description is given by Zephaniah in a series of five couplets. It will be "a day of trouble and distress, a day of waste and desolation, a day of darkness and gloominess, a day of clouds and thick darkness, A day of the trumpet and alarm" (vv. 15-16).

The shrill sound of the battle trumpet mixed with the war cry of the invading hordes filled the populace with anguish and terror. Distress and death so overwhelmed the hemmed-in inhabitants of Jerusalem that they staggered through the city, dazed and helpless, "like blind men" (v. 17). Jerusalem was shrouded in thick, dark smoke, blotting out the hot August sun and suffocating the people in an inferno of total destruction. The nation was completely defenseless against the surging warriors. None of the "fortified cities" or "high towers" (v. 16) stood against the army of Babylon. There was so much carnage that their blood was "poured out like

dust, and their flesh like the dung" (v. 17). The invaders cruelly rav-
ished the bodies of the dead, piling up their internal organs like the
filth of dung hills.[4] All of these things occurred because those who
had "sinned against the LORD" (v. 17) had hardened themselves to
the patient pleading of a loving God, who tried to woo them to
repentance. Now repentance was denied them, and no amount of
"silver nor their gold shall be able to deliver them in the day of the
LORD's wrath" (v. 18). They could not bribe the enemy or God in
order to delay the destruction.

The same is true in the spiritual realm. People cannot be
"redeemed with corruptible things, like silver and gold...But [only]
with the precious blood of Christ, as of a lamb without blemish and
without spot" (1 Pet. 1:18-19). What was true of Judah's destruction will one day be true of the entire world: "the whole land [earth]
shall be devoured by the fire of his [God's] jealousy" (v. 18). When
God's judgment falls, it will bring "a speedy riddance [complete
end] of all those who dwell in the land" (v. 18).

NATIONAL JUDGMENT

Zephaniah pled with Judah to regather before judgment came.
"Gather yourselves together, yea, gather together, O nation not
desired" (2:1). By repeating the phrase, the prophet emphasized
the urgent need for Judah to collectively cry out to God in repentance. The verb *gather* portrays a beggar stooping low to glean
stubble from a field after the main harvest. The word *nation* is used
of Gentiles who do not know God. The phrase *not desired* refers to
people white (pale) with shame, not even blushing before God.
The people of Judah are pictured as worthless, like Gentiles who
have no knowledge of God or shame for their sin, ready to be
destroyed by fire.

There was no time for delay; judgment was coming. Thus,
Zephaniah issued a final call to the nation to repent, introducing

each phrase with the word *before*. Repent "Before the decree bring forth, before the day pass like the chaff" (v. 2). The appointed Day of the Lord had been decreed, and God could bring it to pass as swiftly as chaff is blown away by the wind. Repent "before the fierce anger of the LORD come upon you, before the day of the LORD's anger come upon you" (v. 2)—that is, before the burning anger of God's wrath is poured out in all its fury.

There was within Judah a remnant of people who had remained faithful in their commitment to the Lord. The prophet admonished them to continually "Seek the LORD...seek righteousness, seek meekness" (v. 3). If the faithful remnant continued in righteousness, "it may be [they] shall be hidden in the day of the LORD's anger" (v. 3).

A remnant was hidden (sheltered) from the Day of the Lord's wrath. Many were sent to Babylon in captivity, while "the poorest sort of the people" were permitted to remain in Judah (2 Ki. 24:14-16). Once again, God's grace and mercy were manifested in the midst of judgment. Such will be the case during the Great Tribulation, when the Lord will protect a godly remnant of Jewish believers from the final Day of the Lord (Rev. 7:3-8; 12:13-17).

Although the phrase *Day of the Lord* refers to the local judgment God brought on Judah and its neighboring nations, it also speaks of a future day when God will intervene in the affairs of this world. The Day of the Lord can be described as the direct intervention of God in the affairs of mankind after the Rapture of the church, covering such events as the Tribulation, the Millennial Kingdom, and the Great White Throne Judgment. It is clear from Scripture that this day will not only be a time when God will pour out His wrath upon the wicked, but will also include a time of blessing for Israel and the church during the Millennial reign of Christ on the earth. Peter wrote, "But the day of the Lord will come as a thief in the night, in which the heavens shall pass away with a great noise, and the elements shall melt with fervent heat; the earth also" (2 Pet. 3:10). Because these events will take place after the Millennium, the Day of the Lord will include a time of blessing as well as judgment.

The *Time* magazine reporter may have been right. "The Hour of Doom" may be very near. World events indicate that the Rapture of the church could be near, and the Day of the Lord may soon appear.

At a time such as this, no better warning than Paul's can be given: "Knowing, therefore, the terror of the Lord, we persuade men" (2 Cor. 5:11). We must persuade people that there is a judgment coming on this earth. We must persuade people that they will appear before Christ as their judge. We must persuade people of their need to be reconciled to God through Jesus Christ in light of the coming Day of the Lord.

Zephaniah 2:4-15

For Gaza shall be forsaken, and Ashkelon a desolation; they shall drive out Ashdod at noonday, and Ekron shall be rooted up. Woe unto the inhabitants of the seacoast, the nation of the Cherethites! The word of the LORD is against you; O Canaan, the land of the Philistines, I will even destroy thee, that there shall be no inhabitant. And the seacoast shall be dwellings and cottages for shepherds, and folds for flocks. And the coast shall be for the remnant of the house of Judah; they shall feed there; in the houses of Ashkelon shall they lie down in the evening; for the LORD, their God, shall visit them, and turn away their captivity.

I have heard the reproach of Moab, and the revilings of the children of Ammon, whereby they have reproached my people, and magnified themselves against their border. Therefore, as I live, saith the LORD of hosts, the God of Israel, Surely Moab shall be like Sodom, and the children of Ammon like Gomorrah, even the possession of nettles, and salt pits, and a perpetual desolation; the residue of my people shall spoil them, and the remnant of my people shall possess them. This shall they have for their pride, because they have reproached and magnified themselves against the people of the LORD of hosts. The LORD will be terrible unto them; for he will famish all the gods of the earth; and men shall worship him, every one from his place, even all the coasts of the nations.

Ye Ethiopians also, ye shall be slain by my sword. And he will stretch out his hand against the north, and destroy Assyria; and will make Nineveh a desolation, and dry like a wilderness. And flocks shall lie down in the midst of her, all the beasts of the nations; both the cormorant and the porcupine shall lodge in the upper lintels of it; their voice shall sing in the windows; desolation shall be in the capitals; for he shall uncover the cedar work. This is the rejoicing city that dwelt carelessly, that said in her heart, I am, and there is none beside me. How is she become a desolation, a place for beasts to lie down in! Every one that passeth by her shall hiss, and wag his hand.

THE NATIONS JUDGED

When Iraq's Saddam Hussein invaded neighboring Kuwait, world tensions were ignited. Hussein is a proven despot who envisions himself as a modern-day Nebuchadnezzar and aspires to become the leader of the Muslim world. Such a Herculean feat can be accomplished only by controlling the Middle East oil supply and gaining the support of disenfranchised Arabs throughout the region.

There is biblical precedent for Hussein's aspiration to dominate the Middle East. Both Assyria and Babylon (located in modern-day Iraq) once swept westward to conquer and control the area. Zephaniah detailed how God used Babylon to bring judgment on Gentile nations in the Middle East.

JUDGMENT IN THE WEST

The first area mentioned by Zephaniah is the land known as Palestine before 1948. The word *Palestine* is of Roman origin and refers to the biblical land of the Philistines. The name fell into disuse for centuries but was revived by the British as an official name for the area mandated to their supervision by the League of Nations in 1920. Palestine ceased to exist as a legal entity in 1948, when Great Britain, unable to control Arab-Jewish hostilities, relinquished its mandate to the United Nations. The Israeli state was declared on May 14, 1948.

The Philistines lived in the Mediterranean coastal plains before the time of Abraham (Gen. 20:1ff; 21:22-34; 26:1ff). They were descendants of Ham and came from Caphtor (Jer. 47:4; Amos 9:7), generally thought to be Crete. Philistia had five major cities during Zephaniah's day, four of which he mentioned as being marked out for judgment: Gaza, Ashkelon, Ashdod, and Ekron (v. 4). The fifth city, Gath, was omitted, probably because it had been captured by Uzziah of Judah (2 Chr. 26:6) before this prophecy was given.

Zephaniah said that Gaza would be deserted (v. 4). Gaza was the capital city of the area, and its name means *forsaken*. It was located between Tyre and Egypt on the Mediterranean coast, and the city accumulated great wealth through slave trading.

The Assyrian, Tiglath-pileaser III, attacked Gaza in 743 B.C., making it a vassal city. Pharaoh-neco conquered the city in 609 B.C., and the Babylonians, under Nebuchadnezzar, totally destroyed it around 605 B.C. Through the centuries, Gaza has suffered many defeats.

Today Gaza is the main administration center of what is commonly called the Gaza Strip, a narrow bank of land along the Mediterranean coast, 26 miles long and five miles wide. Its population of approximately 500,000 is composed of refugees from other areas of the region, many living in poverty with little hope of bettering their situation. The Gaza area is a hotbed of unrest, contributing greatly to the Intifada (Palestinian uprising) of the last several years.

Zephaniah went on to prophesy that Ashkelon, which is 12 miles north of Gaza, would become desolate (v. 4). The city was captured by the tribe of Judah (Jud. 1:18) but was subsequently conquered by the Assyrians, Babylonians, Persians, Greeks, Maccabees, and Romans. Jeremiah also declared that Ashkelon would become a wasteland (Jer. 47:5-7).

The prophet also said that Ashdod would be driven out (v. 4). Ashdod is 18 miles northeast of Gaza and was one of the principal ports of Philistia. It was to Ashdod that the Philistines brought the captured Ark of God and put it in the house of Dagon. The next day, Dagon was found on his face before the Ark, having fallen from his pedestal. When the Ark was carried through the city, men were afflicted with tumors (1 Sam. 5:1-9).

The people of Ashdod were to be driven out at "noonday" (v. 4). There are two possible interpretations of this prophecy. Either the siege against the city was to be short, lasting only half a day, or the invaders would strike at noontime when the people were at rest and not on the alert against an attack. The latter view seems most likely. Like other Philistine cities, Ashdod was conquered by most of the great powers already mentioned.

The city of Ekron would be dug up (v. 4). Ekron was a center for the worship of Beelzebub. It was one of the cities promised to the tribe of Judah (Josh. 15:11, 45-46) but was later acquired by the tribe of Dan (Josh. 19:43). It too was conquered by most of the great powers mentioned. Ekron was so completely "rooted up" (v. 4) that there is no trace of it today.

The coastal area of Philistia would be destroyed, including "the inhabitants of the seacoast, the nation of the Cherethites!...Canaan, the land of the Philistines" (v. 5; cp. Jer. 47:4-5; Ezek. 25:15-17). The Cherethites are generally thought to have migrated from Crete to the seacoast of Canaan. Cherethite warriors were part of David's army (2 Sam. 8:18; 20:23; 1 Chr. 18:17). This area too was totally destroyed by the above mentioned armies.

The seacoast would be depopulated and become "dwellings and cottages [caves] for shepherds, and folds for flocks" (v. 6). A "remnant of the house of Judah" would also settle in this area after God had turned "away their captivity" (v. 7) from Babylon. The empty houses of Ashkelon would provide security. The Judeans would "lie down" (v. 7) at night in safety, not having to fear ferocious beasts or evil intruders. This promise was fulfilled in 536 B.C., when Judah returned from the Babylonian captivity. It will be further fulfilled during the Millennium (3:14-20).

JUDGMENT IN THE EAST

Turning from Philistia, Zephaniah looked toward the east and prophesied against Moab and Ammon. Moab and Ammon were sister nations, both descendants of Lot (Gen. 19:30-38), located east of the Jordan River.

God judged them for two reasons. First, He judged them because they "reproached" (v. 8). Israel. Although they were related to Israel, they continually oppressed the nation (Jer. 48:1-49:6; Ezek. 25:1-11). This oppression can be traced back to the time when Balak hired Balaam to curse Israel (Num. 22-24) at the borders of Moab. Even after Israel took possession of the promised land, Moab and Ammon sought to destroy it (Jud. 3:12; 10:7-9; 11:4-6). God used Saul (1 Sam. 11:1-11) and David (2 Sam. 10:1-14) to defeat Ammon, while Jehoram and Jehoshaphat defeated Moab (2 Ki. 3:4-27).

Second, these nations were judged for their pride. They "magnified themselves against their [Israel's] border" (v. 8). They did this in a number of ways.

1. They "reproached" (vv. 8, 10) Israel by their "revilings" (insults and arrogant boastings, v. 8).

2. They tried to retake the land that God gave to Israel.

3. They attempted to domineer Israel.

4. They rebelled against "the LORD of hosts" (v. 10) by trying to destroy His people.

Amos revealed two other sins for which these nations were judged. First, the Ammonites "ripped up" pregnant women during their border raids into Gilead, thus destroying the country's population and making it impossible to extend their land holdings (Amos 1:13). Second, the Moabites committed the despicable crime of digging up the bones of Edom's king and burning them into lime (Amos 2:1). Although this incident is not recorded in the historical books, many scholars believe it occurred during the time when Edom aligned itself with King Jehoram of Israel and King Jehoshaphat of Judah to attack King Mesha of Moab (2 Ki. 3:4-9).

The pronouncement of God's judgment was given: "Surely Moab shall be like Sodom, and the children of Ammon like Gomorrah" (v. 9). These nations were to meet the same utter destruction as the two cities from which their parents had been delivered. Their land would be overgrown with "nettles" (thorns and thistles, v. 9), a symbol of judgment and desolation (cp. Isa. 34:13; Hos. 9:6; 10:8). The land would be covered with "salt pits" (v. 9), thus becoming salty like the area surrounding Sodom and Gomorrah. It would be a "perpetual desolation" (v. 9). The once-fertile lands of Moab and Ammon would become sterile, salty, and desolate, with no hope of recovery. The certainty of their destruction is affirmed by the words, "as I live, saith the LORD of hosts" (v. 9). Jehovah swore by Himself (because there is no higher authority) that both nations would be completely destroyed. Finally, their land would be possessed by Israel: "the residue of my people shall spoil them, and the remnant of my people shall possess them" (v. 9). This prophecy will be fulfilled during the Millennium, when Israel occupies the land promised to them in the Abrahamic Covenant.

The Lord has shown Himself to be "terrible" (v. 11) to Moab and Ammon as an example to all people around the world and throughout the ages who practice idolatry: "for he will famish all the gods of the earth; and men shall worship him" (v. 11). God will ultimately destroy idolatry worldwide, leaving only Himself to be worshiped. Worship of God alone will become a reality during the Millennium (Mic. 4:1-2; Zech. 14:16; Mal. 1:11).

Ammon and Moab, which were located in the area known today as Jordan, were defeated at the hands of nations more powerful than themselves when the Philistine cities were destroyed. History confirms that Moab ceased to be a power in the Middle East.

JUDGMENT IN THE SOUTH

Zephaniah then turned from the east to the south and prophesied judgment on the Ethiopians. "Ye Ethiopians also, ye shall be slain by my sword," said the Lord. (v. 12; cp. Isa. 20:4; Ezek. 30:4-9). Ethiopia is southwest of Egypt and was inhabited by the Cushites. They were descendants of Ham (Gen. 10:6) and controlled the area known as Eastern Sudan, Ethiopia, Somalia, and Eritrea. The Ethiopians ruled Egypt from 720-654 B.C., and at times they threatened Judah (2 Ki. 19:9; 2 Chr. 14:9-13; Isa. 37:9).

Ethiopia's destruction is simply stated: "ye shall be slain by my sword" (v. 12). The sword referred to is the Babylonians, whom God used, under the leadership of Nebuchadnezzar, to destroy Ethiopia in 586 B. C. (Ezek. 30:4-5, 9).

The Ethiopians will be confederated with the army from the north that will invade Israel during the Tribulation (Ezek. 38:5). Still, the Lord is concerned about the salvation of Ethiopia and will include it in the Millennium (3:10).

JUDGMENT IN THE NORTH

Turning from the south, Zephaniah looked toward the north and prophesied the destruction of Assyria. Although Assyria was situated northwest of Judah, the prophet spoke of the nation as being north (v. 13) because it was from that direction that it invaded Israel. Assyria dominated the ancient world from 883-612 B.C., but Zephaniah prophesied that the Lord would "destroy Assyria; and...make Nineveh a desolation, and dry like a wilderness" (v. 13).

Nineveh was situated on the left bank of the Tigris River opposite present-day Mosual, Iraq. It seemed to be an impregnable city, being more than 7.5 miles long and encompassing an area of 1,730 acres—enough territory to accommodate 120,000 people. Its walls were 10 feet high and 50 feet wide and had 1,200 protective towers and 15 gates. The king's palace had at least 80 rooms with 9,880 feet of sculptured walls detailing his victories in battle. The king boasted of a library containing more than 20,000 clay tablets dealing with such subjects as religion, science, and lexicography. Within the city were parks, botanical gardens with unusual plants, and a zoo. Water was supplied through conduits from approximately 25 miles away. They even constructed an aqueduct to control flooding from rivers in the area.

The destruction of Nineveh came at the hands of the Medes

and Babylonians, after a two-month siege, in August of 612 B.C. Historians state that its overthrow was due, in part, to a sudden release of dammed-up water that surged against the city wall. This, in turn, softened the sun-dried brick wall, making it easy for the invading armies to break through and capture the city (Nah. 1:8; 2:6; 3:13, 15). Nineveh's destruction was so complete that Alexander the Great marched his army over the buried city and never knew it. The city became utterly desolate, as the prophet had declared, being occupied only by wild beasts such as the cormorant (pelican)—an unclean bird (Lev. 11:17)—and the porcupine (v. 14). The phrase "their voice" (v. 14) refers to the wind making a sighing or moaning noise as it blows through an open window or door in the desolate city. The sound over Nineveh was like a funeral dirge.

Zephaniah profiled Assyria's attitude before its destruction. First, its prosperity produced a self-indulgent lifestyle, giving it the image of a "rejoicing city" (v. 15). Second, its power and protection made it feel secure and invincible, thus, it "dwelt carelessly" (v. 15), giving no thought to the possibility of being conquered. Third, it became proud in its position, boasting, "I am, and there is none beside me" (v. 15). Such is the boast of nations, both ancient and modern, at the height of their power (cp. Isa. 47:10). God will not only bring such nations to "desolation," but He will cause those who pass by to "hiss, and wag his hand" (v. 15). People will scoff and shake their fists at Assyria as a sign of contempt for a nation that considered itself better than others.

This age-old scenario is once again being played out as Iraq's Saddam Hussein flexes his military might, saying, "I am, and there is none beside me in the Middle East!" Iraq's unprovoked attack against defenseless Kuwait in August 1990 raised the ire of nations worldwide. They drew a line in the sand, warning that further Iraqi aggression would precipitate a full-scale war in the region. Between

August and November, the United Nations Security Council passed a series of resolutions that culminated in the demand that Iraq withdraw unconditionally from Kuwait by January 15, 1991. Saddam Hussein refused, and within 24 hours after the United Nations deadline expired, a multinational coalition began intensive aerial bombardment of military targets in Iraq. Within one hundred hours, the United Nations coalition, under the command of U. S. General H. Norman Schwartzkoff, had liberated Kuwait. When the offensive operation was suspended on February 26, 1991, tens of thousands of Iraqi troops had deserted, surrendered, been captured, or were killed.

God's Word is sure: Judgment will inevitably come to the Middle East in the areas described by Zephaniah's prophecy. But just when that judgment will take place is uncertain. Could it be that the world-shaking events we are witnessing daily in Eastern Europe and the Middle East indicate that the stage is being set for the fulfillment of end-time prophecy? Recent world events give indication that we are on the threshold of seeing biblical prophecy come to fruition.

Zephaniah 3:1-8

Woe to her that is filthy and polluted, to the oppressing city! She obeyed not the voice; she received not correction; she trusted not in the LORD; she drew not near to her God. Her princes within her are roaring lions; her judges are evening wolves; they gnaw not the bones till the morrow. Her prophets are light and treacherous persons; her priests have polluted the sanctuary, they have done violence to the law. The just LORD is in the midst of her; he will not do iniquity; every morning doth he bring his justice to light, he faileth not; but the unjust knoweth no shame. I have cut off the nations, their towers are desolate; I made their streets waste, that none passeth by; their cities are destroyed, so that there is no man, that there is no inhabitant. I said, Surely thou wilt fear me, thou wilt receive instruction; so their dwelling should not be cut off, however I punished them; but they rose early, and corrupted all their doings.

Therefore, wait upon me, saith the LORD, until the day that I rise up to the prey; for my determination is to gather the nations, that I may assemble the kingdoms, to pour upon them mine indignation, even all my fierce anger; for all the earth shall be devoured with the fire of my jealousy.

JUDGMENT ON JERUSALEM

Perhaps no city on earth is more loved than Jerusalem. The psalmist has well written, "Beautiful for situation, the joy of the whole earth, is Mount Zion…the city of the great King" (Ps. 48:2). God said, "This is Jerusalem; I have set her in the midst of the nations and countries that are round about her" (Ezek. 5:5). Moses, the great lawgiver, said that when God gave the nations their boundaries, He did so in relationship to Israel (Dt. 32:8). Jerusalem is the city of God, the capital of Judah, the sanctuary of spiritual life, and the joy of the whole earth to the Jew.

Never could Jerusalem's princes or people envision its destruction, especially by its heathen neighbors. Here only had God placed His name and revealed His law to the world. Here only was God truly worshiped. And here only stood the great Temple of Solomon, wherein dwelt God's Shekinah glory.

But the stench of Jerusalem's moral depravity had reached the nostrils of the holy God. He no longer could tolerate the defamation of His holy name, the pollution of His sanctuary, and the oppression of the righteous. In graphic language, Zephaniah detailed Jerusalem's corruption and its soon-coming judgment.

WOE TO THE CITY

Zephaniah continued his prophecy against Judah with a strong condemnation of Jerusalem: "Woe to her that is filthy and polluted" (v. 1). Not only was Jerusalem defiled, but it had become defiant toward God. "She obeyed not the voice" of God (v. 2), choosing instead to turn a deaf ear to the prophets' warnings of imminent judgment. "She received not correction" (v. 2), ignoring the lessons suffered by the ten tribes of Israel and those of its own history. "She trusted not in the LORD" (v. 2) but put her faith in heathen gods, military power, her own cunning wisdom, and alliances with pagan nations. "She drew not near to her God" (v. 2), asking to be forgiven of sin and guided toward renewal. The nation had become corrupt and lacked a true desire to commune with God.

Jerusalem's defilement led to its degradation, and it became known as the "oppressing city" (v. 1). When a city ignores God's law and turns to rampant immorality, oppression results throughout every level of society, from the rich to the poor. Isaiah recorded that the people were being "oppressed, every one by another, and every one by his neighbor," and the children were behaving "proudly against the ancient [elderly], and the base against the honorable" (Isa. 3:5).

Worthless cults and customs had flooded in from the East. Wealth gleaned through oppression filled the land. The nation was replete with idols; the people were worshiping the works of their own hands (Isa. 2:6-8). Even their facial expressions witnessed against them; they declared their sin like Sodom (Isa. 3:9). They had become totally corrupt from the tops of their heads to the soles of their feet (Isa. 1:5-6).

Lest we be quick to pass judgment on Jerusalem, consider the conditions existing in many major American cities. God's Word has been rejected, and the warning of coming judgment receives little attention. In fact, for the most part, it goes unheeded. People are trusting in Eastern philosophy and the gods of military power and alliances with nations whose records on human rights are deplorable. The sin of Sodom is showing on the countenances of many throughout this country, as homosexuals parade for gay rights. Oppression between neighbors is rampant. In this country there is a burglary every 10 seconds, a larceny every 2.5 minutes, a rape every 19 minutes, and a murder every 27 minutes. This author and his wife have been robbed three times in the past 22 years. *Woe to America!* is the warning from God.

WICKED CITIZENS

Zephaniah denounced the leaders of Jerusalem as ruthless despots who cared only for their own interests. Its princes were pictured as "roaring lions" (v. 3). Princes were put into positions of power to maintain peace and provide protection for the people. But these princes abused their positions by moving throughout Judah's society like voracious and violent lions, preying on vulnerable victims (cp. Prov. 28:15-16). They used unrestrained power to satisfy their passion for wealth. It is God who puts people in positions of authority (Dan. 2:21), and they are expected to carry out their responsibilities with justice and in the fear of God (2 Sam. 23:3).

A nation cannot function properly without a power structure, but power in the hands of a ruthless dictator will, in the long run, be the instrument of a nation's undoing. Modern-day dictators—such as Hitler, Stalin, and Mao-Tse-tung—have exacted a heavy toll on their countries, leaving them financially and socially diminished or destroyed. Satan, working through despotic princes, goes throughout a country seeking whom he may devour (1 Pet. 5:8). Political oppression of the people by Judah's leadership was one of the major reasons for God's destruction of the country.

Zephaniah described Judah's judges as "evening wolves" (v. 3). These judges or magistrates should have protected the poor, indigent, and innocent within their country. Instead, they aided and abetted injustice through political oppression (cp. Amos 2:6-8; Hab. 1:8).

Wolves are clever, wily, ferocious, and merciless, always on the lookout for new victims. Like evening wolves—who slide in under the cover of darkness to grab an unsuspecting prey and greedily gulp it down—so these judges—under the pretense of law and justice—rapaciously gobbled up the wealth and property of those who came before them. They were like wolves who, deprived of food, comb vast areas looking for a meal at great risk to their own lives. The prophet said, "they gnaw not the bones till the morrow" (v. 3). They gulped down their prey, and there was nothing left the next morning. Like lawless wolves, these leaders used the law to their own advantage to accumulate wealth.

Micah is very descriptive concerning abuse by Judah's leaders. He wrote that the people were treated like cattle to be eaten. The leaders stripped off their skin, broke their bones in pieces, and chopped them up like meat to be fried in a pan or boiled in a pot (Mic. 3:3).

Amos explained how social injustice was perpetrated on the poor. The judges perverted justice by selling "the righteous for silver" (Amos 2:6)—that is, the judges condemned righteous people for a bribe, or possibly sold into slavery those who would not or could not pay their debts. This was not legal in Israel (Lev. 25:39). The poor were sold "for a pair of shoes" (Amos 2:6)—almost nothing. These cruel creditors "pant[ed] after the dust of the earth on the head of the poor" (Amos 2:7). They oppressed the poor so severely that when the poor mourned by casting dust on themselves, the leaders even removed the dust that they had placed on their heads in their misery. These heartless leaders did everything within their power to destroy the judicial process of the courts, especially regarding their creditors. Jerusalem's judges were so corrupt that they were hastening the city's demise.

The foundation of any society is the integrity of its judicial system. When the courts become so degraded that injustice, rather than justice, is meted out, society is on the brink of total decline.

Judah's prophets are described as "light and treacherous persons" (v. 4)—"light" in the sense of being shallow, superficial, frivolous, and irresponsible in their prophecies. Thus, they were "treacherous," deceiving the people by posing as true messengers from God, all the while exploiting their position for personal and financial gain. Many were drunkards, profane and wicked men who lived immoral lives and practiced divination. They were religious opportunists who hired themselves out (Mic. 3:11), giving a corrupt people the kind of message they wanted to hear (Isa. 30:10-12; Mic. 2:11), a message of peace and prosperity (Jer. 14:13; 23:17; Ezek. 13:1-16).[1]

The priests abused their office in two ways. They "polluted the sanctuary" (v. 4) by offering defective animals, a practice strictly forbidden by law (Lev. 22:17-30), and they did not wash their hands or change their clothing after each offering. This automatically disqualified them as unclean to perform their priestly functions. They also did "violence to the law" (v. 4) by not teaching its precepts to the people or following its principles in the execution of justice.

Judah was without excuse for its perversity because it had daily reminders of God's holiness.

1. It had "The just LORD...in the midst of her" (v. 5). His Shekinah glory filling Solomon's Temple was a continual sign and reminder of His holiness and righteousness to the nation.

2. God is perfect; it is impossible for Him to do iniquity (v. 5) or tolerate it in His presence. A holy God must act in harmony with His nature and character (Dt. 32:4).

3. His righteousness was a daily reminder to Judah that "every morning [lit., morning by morning] doth he bring his justice to light" (v. 5). God's righteousness and justice were shown through the daily sacrifices, which revealed His judgment against sin and pointed people to their need of redemption.

4. He showed justice through the daily proclamation of the righteous prophets who warned the nation to turn from sin (Jer. 7:25-28).

5. He showed justice through the daily reading and teaching of the law. God did not fail to consistently keep His righteousness before the people as a reminder of their responsibility to Him.

But this daily witness had little effect on the nation. The people became so callous to the righteousness of God in their midst that they knew no shame (v. 5). Their seared consciences had no sense of shame or conviction when their sin was pointed out to them (Jer. 6:15).

The same can be said of America today. God's righteousness is manifested daily in our nation via radio, television, pulpits, and the printed page. Yet the people have become callous and pay little attention to the call for righteous living. Although many claim to believe in God and attend church services each Sunday, few make a serious attempt to turn from sin and live a holy life.

WARNING TO THE CITY

God had warned Judah that failure to serve Him in righteousness would bring about its destruction. The nation had many examples of God's warning. He had cut off the surrounding nations (v. 6)—who committed gross sin—through Joshua's conquest of the land of Canaan and again in 722 B.C., when the Assyrians destroyed the northern ten tribes of Israel. Their towers (v. 6) proved to be an inadequate defense against the invading nations. Their streets and cities had been leveled, leaving them without inhabitants (v. 6). The words of Moses were an even stronger reminder, as they detailed the awesome judgment the people would experience if they failed to obey God (Lev. 26; Dt. 28).

God reasoned, "Surely thou [Judah] wilt fear me, thou wilt receive instruction" (v. 7). He wanted the Israelites to learn the lessons of history, "so their dwelling [nation] should not be cut off" and the appointed punishment would not come (v. 7). Such a vivid reminder should have awakened the city to repentance, but it was not to be. The people were stubborn and closed their eyes to God's warnings. They refused to believe that the Lord would destroy the place where He had chosen to put His name.

The nation was so totally absorbed in sin that the people rose early (v. 7), eager to commit iniquity. They tried to squeeze as much sin out of the day as they could. They were so committed to corruption that it became an obsession. Everything they did was evil—so much so that their "doings" were against the Lord (v. 7). The word *doings* means *mighty works* and refers to the great crimes the people committed in the sight of God.[2] For such a privileged people to become so engulfed in iniquity is mind-boggling.

WORLDWIDE CONDEMNATION

In the midst of judgment, God provided a word of hope to a righteous remnant of Jews within the nation. The Lord said, "wait upon me" (v. 8). They were to wait and not lose hope during the time of judgment, when all seemed lost. The remnant who waited in Zephaniah's day prefigured a remnant of Jews whom God will supernaturally protect through the Tribulation period and deliver when Christ returns (Rev. 7:4-8; 12:6, 17).

God, in His own time, would "rise up to the prey" (v. 8) like a mighty hunter. The *prey* refers to the wicked people in Judah and the surrounding nations, whose judgment prefigured God's judgment on the world during the Great Tribulation. God would rise up at the proper time and demonstrate His justice by springing on these wicked nations and destroying them like a savage beast, hungry for its prey.

God had determined to gather the nations (v. 8) to Jerusalem for the sole purpose of pouring out His indignation and fierce anger on them (v. 8; cp. Ps. 2:1-5, 9; Zech. 14:12; Rev. 16:14; 19:15). The Great Tribulation will be so awesome in its destruction that "all the earth shall be devoured with the fire of [God's] jealousy" (v. 8). In that day, there will be no doubt concerning God's abhorrence of sin and the fact that He alone reigns in righteousness over creation.

There is a spirit of expectancy among Christians everywhere—expectancy of soon-coming judgment against America unless there is a turning from the moral, social, and religious decay that has so gripped this country—expectancy that the puzzle of end-time prophecy is on the table, and the pieces are slowly being moved into place toward the completion of the puzzle—expectancy that Christ's return for His own is imminent. In light of this hope, there must be an awakening to holy living.

Are you prepared, my friend?

Zephaniah 3:9-20

For then will I turn to the peoples a pure language, that they may all call upon the name of the LORD, to serve him with one consent. From beyond the rivers of Ethiopia my suppliants, even the daughter of my dispersed, shall bring mine offering. In that day shalt thou not be ashamed for all thy doings, in which thou hast transgressed against me; for then I will take away out of the midst of thee those who rejoice in thy pride, and thou shalt no more be haughty in my holy mountain. I will also leave in the midst of thee an afflicted and poor people, and they shall trust in the name of the LORD. The remnant of Israel shall not do iniquity, nor speak lies, neither shall a deceitful tongue be found in their mouth; for they shall feed and lie down, and none shall make them afraid.

Sing, O daughter of Zion; shout, O Israel; be glad and rejoice with all the heart, O daughter of Jerusalem. The LORD hath taken away thy judgments, he hath cast out thine enemy; the King of Israel, even the LORD, is in the midst of thee, thou shalt not see evil any more. In that day it shall be said to Jerusalem, Fear thou not; and to Zion, Let not thine hands be slack. The LORD, thy God, in the midst of thee is mighty; he will save, he will rejoice over thee with joy; he will rest in his love, he will joy over thee with singing. I will gather those who are sorrowful for the solemn assembly, who are of thee, to whom the reproach of it was a burden. Behold, at that time I will undo all that afflict thee; and I will save her that is lame, and gather her that was driven out; and I will get them praise and fame in every land where they have been put to shame. At that time will I bring you again, even in the time that I gather you; for I will make you a name and a praise among all peoples of the earth, when I turn back your captivity before your eyes, saith the LORD.

THE MESSIANIC KINGDOM

Hope ran high that the decade of the 1990s would usher in world peace. The buzz phrase of the day was "Peace in our time." With the sudden invasion of Kuwait by Saddam Hussein, such dreams came to a screeching halt. Instead of peace, the world braced itself for war in the Middle East. A war-wearied world fixed its eyes on Iraq, silently questioning whether world peace would ever become a reality.

Scripture is replete with prophecies declaring that world peace will become a reality—but not until Jesus Christ, "The Prince of Peace" (Isa. 9:6), returns to the earth to establish His promised Kingdom. With this hope in mind, Zephaniah penned his final message of encouragement to Judah. In graphic detail, the prophet described what it will be like for Israel and the world when the Messianic Kingdom becomes a universal reality.

REDEMPTION IN THE KINGDOM

Only those who have been redeemed will be permitted to enter the Kingdom age. Scripture indicates that they will be given renewed speech: "For then will I turn to the peoples a pure language, that they may all call upon the name of the LORD, to serve him with one consent" (v. 9).

Some scholars have interpreted the words *pure language* to mean that Hebrew will become the universal language in the Kingdom. They hold this view for four reasons.

1. The Lord will be ruling from Jerusalem, the capital city of the world, where "they may all call upon the name of the LORD."

2. Because Jerusalem will be the city to which the nations will come to learn about and worship the Lord, it is logical to assume that they will speak Hebrew.

3. The unity of language anticipates the fulfillment of Joel's prophecy, which speaks of the Holy Spirit being poured out on all people (Joel 2:28-29) and may facilitate the spread of the knowledge of the Lord, as predicted by Habakkuk (Hab. 2:14).[1]

4. God confused the languages of the nations because of pagan worship. The curse of Babel, which divided people and caused their scattering, will be removed, allowing them to worship the Lord with one language.

Although this interpretation is held by many, it does not seem to be the meaning of verse 9. The word *turn* means to *restore* and refers to changing the nature of corrupt speech into a language that is pure. This means that the converted people who enter the Kingdom will be purified from their idolatry and blasphemy against God. The promise of Joel 2:28-29 will be fulfilled when God pours out

His Spirit on all flesh during the Kingdom age, which will produce a pure language but not a universal language.

Jewish believers, referred to as "the daughter of my dispersed," will return to Jerusalem from "beyond the rivers of Ethiopia" (v. 10), which is the upper Nile region of southern Egypt, Sudan, and northern Ethiopia. Both Jewish and Gentile believers will bring offerings (v. 10) to present to the Lord when they come. The offering (Heb., *minchan*) mentioned in this passage is the meal offering.

Bringing offerings to the Lord presupposes rebuilding the Temple and reinstituting the sacrificial system during the Millennial Kingdom. There are many similarities between the Aaronic and Millennial systems. In the Millennial system:

1. Worship centers in an altar (Ezek. 43:13-17), where blood is sprinkled (43:18), and burnt, sin, trespass (40:39), and meal offerings (42:13) are presented.

2. The Levitical order is reinstituted through the priestly ministry of Zadok (43:19).

3. There are prescribed rituals of cleansing for the altar (43:20-27), the Levites who minister (44:25-27), and the sanctuary (45:18).

4. New moon and Sabbath days will be observed (46:1).

5. Morning sacrifice will be offered daily (46:13).

6. The feasts of Passover (45:21-24) and Tabernacles (45:25) will be celebrated annually, along with the year of Jubilee at its proper time (46:17).

7. There is a similarity in the regulations given to govern the manner of life, dress, and priestly order (44:15-31).

8. The Millennial Temple will be the place in which this ministry will be performed and the glory of God will be manifested (43:4-5).

Thus, worship in the Millennium will bear a strong similarity to the old Aaronic order.[2]

The question is often raised, *If Jesus' sacrifice was the only efficacious, once-for-all sacrifice to expiate sin, why should animal sacrifices, which could never take away sin, be offered during the Millennium?* It is true that the sacrifices in the Millennial Temple will not expiate sin, just as the Mosaic offerings could not. Many conservative commentators conclude that these offerings will be memorial in nature, similar to the church in this age keeping the Lord's supper in remembrance of Christ's death. The offerings will be a visible reminder of Christ's efficacious work on the cross. Although this is true, it would seem that the sacrifices during the Millennium will have an added function. They will be offered "to make reconciliation [atonement] for the house of Israel" (Ezek. 45:17; see vv. 15, 20). This is not a return to the Old Testament Mosaic Covenant or law. It is a whole new system set up by the Lord with dispensational distinctives that are applicable to the Millennial Kingdom. Remember, the Millennial system is based on the Abrahamic Covenant, the Palestinian Covenant, and the Davidic Covenant— not the Mosaic Covenant.

In the Old Testament, the word *atonement* means *a covering.* The Levitical system showed people the hideousness of their sinful condition and the need to cover their sins with a blood sacrifice. As mentioned previously, the blood atonement never took away sin. When the people made atonement, they were simply covering their sins, averting God's divine anger and punishment by paying a ransom. It was Christ's death on the cross, not the Levitical system, that made it possible for people's sins to be taken away.

In like manner, the animal sacrifices offered during the Millennium will serve primarily to remove ceremonial uncleanness and prevent defilement from polluting the Temple envisioned by Ezekiel. This will be needed because the glorious presence of God will once again dwell on the earth in the midst of sinful people. This purging act propitiated God, thus enabling Him to dwell among His people. The atonement cleansing was necessary in Leviticus because of the descent of the Shekinah glory in Exodus 40. The holy God had taken up residence in the midst of sinful and unclean people. Similarly, Ezekiel foresaw the return of God's glory to the Millennial Temple. The important point is that uncleanness was treated as a contagion that had to be washed away lest it cause defilement. The future animal sacrifices will not deal with matters of eternal salvation, but with finite cleansing of impurities from people living in the Millennial Kingdom in their natural bodies. The Millennial Kingdom sacrifices will not diminish Christ's work on the cross or violate a literal interpretation of the sacrifices.[3]

At the beginning of the Kingdom age, God will remove the shame of Israel. "In that day" the redeemed of Israel will "not be ashamed" (v. 11). The sinful "doings" (lit., *terrible deeds*) that brought Israel to shame will be taken "out of [its] midst" (v. 11). Those who are proud and haughty will be purged out (v. 11) when God judges Israel and the Gentile nations at Christ's return. Only the righteous will inhabit the Lord's "holy mountain" (Jerusalem, v. 11).

The remnant of submissive people who "trust in the name of the LORD" is described as being "afflicted and poor" (v. 12). This does not mean that they are diseased and poverty-stricken, but humble in spirit. The attitude of pride and arrogance will be removed from those residing in the land, and their appearance will reflect a serene trust in God.

Holiness will characterize redeemed sinners. Their conduct will be upright, for they "shall not do iniquity" (v. 13). They will not practice fraud or double-dealing in their relationships with others. Their conversation will be pure; they will not "speak lies, neither shall a deceitful tongue be found in their mouth" (v. 13). The word *lies* probably refers to religious lies associated with idolatrous worship, which characterized the false prophets. The cleansed remnant will be comforted: "for they shall feed and lie down, and none shall make them afraid" (v. 13). The redeemed of Israel are compared to a flock of sheep led and tended by the Lord, their Shepherd. They will no longer be afraid of the oppressor who comes to destroy them, for they will lie down in security and comfort and feed on the truth and righteousness provided by the Lord. This is the fulfillment of promises made in the Shepherd Psalm (Ps. 23).

REJOICING IN THE KINGDOM

The redeemed are encouraged to rejoice in song at the news of their deliverance. They are to "Sing…shout…be glad and rejoice with all the heart" (v. 14). Three names are used for Israel in calling the nation to rejoice in song: "daughter of Zion…Israel…daughter of Jerusalem" (v. 14). This is a personification of the 12 tribes of Israel, who will again be united in the land during the Kingdom age.

Israel's rejoicing will be centered in Christ's return because "The LORD hath taken away [its] judgments" (v. 15; cp. vv. 1-7). Judicially, Israel had been sentenced for its crimes against God and mankind. They had been doubly disciplined for their sins (Isa. 40:2), and now the charges against the nation would be forgiven.

Israel will rejoice because the Lord has "cast out [its] enemy" (v. 15). The nations that persecute Israel will no longer be a threat to its survival, for they will receive their judgment from the hand of God—especially those who come against Israel during the Great

Tribulation (Zech. 14:2-3, 12-15).

Israel will rejoice because "the LORD, is in the midst" of it (v. 15). Christ's return can be described as the personal, visible, physical return of the Lord to the earth in power and great glory, with His angels and saints, to fulfill His covenant promises to Israel and the church. What a great day of rejoicing that will be!

Israel will rejoice because the nation need "not see [fear] evil any more" (v. 15). During the Kingdom age, evil will not be openly manifested because Satan will be bound in the bottomless pit (Rev. 20:2-3), and Christ will reign on the earth with "a rod of iron" (Rev. 12:5). It will be a time when peace fills the earth (Isa. 66:12).

Israel will rejoice over the encouragement received from nations around the world, who will say two things to Israel:

1. "Fear thou not" (v. 16), or take courage, for your judgment is past, your enemies are destroyed, and the Lord, who dwells in your presence, guarantees your peace and security.

2. "Zion" don't let your "hands be slack" (v. 16), a sign of discouragement, despair, and lack of energy and productivity. There will be no need for such despondency and listlessness because the Lord will deliver them and provide peace, prosperity, and productivity.

RESTORATION IN THE KINGDOM

Zephaniah went on to provide Israel with a number of reasons why they should feel secure and comforted. First, the nation could take comfort in the presence of the Lord: "The LORD, thy God, [is] in the midst of thee" (v. 17). For centuries, Jewish people have taken hope and comfort in the promise that the Messiah will one day come and bring world peace, secure the land of Israel for them, and rebuild the Temple on its historic site in Jerusalem. Zephaniah assured Israel that Christ will one day be visibly present in His glorious person to fulfill all the promises He has made to the nation.

Second, the nation can take comfort in protection from the Lord, for He is "mighty; he will save" (v. 17). The Lord is the all-powerful one who will guarantee the preservation and deliverance of Israel from any person or peril that threatens the nation's safety in the Kingdom age. One writer notes that Zephaniah described the Lord as Israel's mighty *gibbor*, "valiant warrior," *yoshia*, "who saves" or "who is victorious." The picture is of Boaz (*ish gibbor hayil*, "mighty man of valor"), who redeemed Ruth from poverty and distress. In fulfilling the role of a kinsman-redeemer, he took her as his bride and rejoiced over her. She, on her part, entered into the "rest of his love."[4]

The nation can take comfort in the pleasure of the Lord, for He will rejoice over them with joy (v 17). His rejoicing is due to the spiritual return of the nation to a place of holiness as a chaste and comely bride (Isa. 62:5; Jer. 32:41; Hos. 2:19).

The nation can take comfort in God's perfect love, for "he will rest in his love" for the nation (v. 17). The word *rest* means to be *silent* and denotes a love so deeply felt and absorbed in its object, with thoughtfulness and admiration, that it need not be demonstrated.[5]

The nation can take comfort in God's praise over it, for He will "joy over [them] with singing" (v. 17). The Lord will not remain silent concerning His indescribable love for Israel and its renewed relationship with Him. He will sing with delight and joy, as one would sing in a day of festival, because His people Israel will be in the land enjoying the Kingdom blessings promised to them. This is also true of God's love for His church. He has loved His own to the end and takes great joy in them.

REASSURANCE IN THE KINGDOM

Zephaniah closed his prophecy on a note of reassurance to the nation of Judah. Although it would soon be destroyed by Babylon, God would not utterly forsake it because He is committed to the nation's ultimate deliverance. He assured Israel of His love with six *I wills* in verses 18 to 20.

1. God cares for all Jewish people in the Diaspora and says, "*I will* gather those who are sorrowful for the solemn assembly" (v. 18). These people have been exiled and are grieving because they are unable to attend their sacred feasts in Israel. They will be returned to Israel and will once again take part in these religious observances.

2. God said, "*I will* undo all that afflict thee" (v. 19). He will destroy those who oppressed Israel at the time of its deliverance. In the Abrahamic Covenant, God promised that He would "bless them that bless thee [Israel], and curse him [its enemies] that curseth thee" (Gen. 12:3). This promise has been fulfilled many times through the centuries and will be fulfilled again when Christ destroys Israel's enemies at His return.

3. God said, "*I will* save her that is lame, and gather her that was driven out" (v. 19). Those who are hurt, homeless, and helpless will be healed and given new homes in the Promised Land.

4. God said, "*I will* get them praise and fame in every land where they have been put to shame" (v. 19). No longer will they be objects of shame, but objects of praise. The nations will marvel at how God has gifted and blessed His people. Not only will the nations be awestruck at the fame of the Jewish people, but also at how God has worked on their behalf to bless and prosper them.

5. God said, "At that time *will I* bring you again, even in the time that I gather you" (v. 20). The Lord repeated the promise that Israel would be gathered back to its land after the Great Tribulation to emphasize His commitment to accomplish this promise.

6. God said, "for *I will* make you a name and a praise among all peoples of the earth" (v. 20). Today, Israel is still a reproach among the nations of the world, as evidenced by frequent actions taken by the United Nations in their voting, as well as by national groups in Eastern Europe that continually persecute the Jewish population within their borders. But after Israel's cleansing, "God will set [it] on high above all nations of the earth" (Dt. 28:1; cp. Dt. 26:19; 28:13), and the nations will praise it. Israel will be blessed when Christ restores the nation at His Second Coming. One third of the Jewish population will survive the Great Tribulation and will become the "all Israel" mentioned in Romans 11:26 that will witness this taking place.

Amillennialists continually deny that these promises are yet to be fulfilled to a nationally restored Israel during the Kingdom age. But Scripture provides irrefutable evidence that such an interpretation of the biblical record is incorrect. The promise of Israel's restoration and spiritual renewal is repeated more than 140 times in Scripture.

The certainty of such a spiritual and physical restoration is guaranteed by the divine authority of the Lord, for Zephaniah concluded his prophecy with the words, "saith the LORD" (v. 20).

When Zephaniah wrote his prophecy, a neo-Babylonian empire had risen to great power and was soon to destroy little

Israel. Twenty-six hundred years later, little has changed. Another neo-Babylonian empire has emerged and once again threatens to annihilate Israel. But this time it will not be successful; Israel will survive.

We are living in the latter days in which the nation of Israel is to play a strategic role, for it must be a sovereign nation when the Tribulation begins, after which it will enjoy the Kingdom blessings foretold by Zephaniah. The eyes of the world remain glued on the Middle East, and it seems certain that there will not be the "peace in our time" for which the world longs.

War will come again in the future. Jesus said there is coming a time of tribulation on the earth "such as was not since the beginning of the world to this time, no, nor ever shall be" (Mt. 24:21). He also warned those living during the time of the Great Tribulation to "be...ready; for in such an hour as ye think not the Son of man cometh" (Mt. 24:44).

ENDNOTES

CHAPTER 1

[1] John D. Hannah, *The Bible Knowledge Commentary, Zephaniah* (Wheaton: Victor Books, 1985), p. 1523.

[2] Theo Laetsch, *The Minor Prophets, Zephaniah* (St. Louis: Concordia Publishing House, 1956), p. 355.

[3] Cyril J. Barber, *Everyman's Bible Commentary, Habakkuk and Zephaniah* (Chicago: Moody Press, 1985), p. 91.

[4] Merrill F. Unger, *Unger's Bible Dictionary, Ashtoreth* (Chicago: Moody Press, 1957), pp. 412-13.

[5] John Ankerberg and John Weldon, *The Facts on Astrology* (Eugene: Harvest House Publishers, Inc., 1988), pp. 8-10.

[6] John Ankerberg and John Weldon, *The Facts on the Occult* (Eugene: Harvest House Publishers, Inc., 1991), p. 8.

[7] John Ankerberg and John Weldon, *The Facts on the New Age Movement* (Eugene: Harvest House Publishers, Inc. 1988), p. 8.

[8] Unger, *op. cit.*, p. 488.

[9] John Ankerberg and John Weldon, *The Facts on the Masonic Lodge* (Eugene, Harvest House Publishers, Inc., 1989), p. 31.

[10] T. Wilson Litzenberger, *Startling Trends in Our Generation, Religion* (Broadview: Gibbs Publishing, 1974), pp. 172-73.

CHAPTER 2

[1] Theo Laetsch, *The Minor Prophets, Zephaniah* (St. Louis, Concordia Publishing House, 1956), p. 362.

[2] Frederick A. Tatford, *The Minor Prophets, Zephaniah*, (Minneapolis: Klock and Klock Christian Publishers, Inc., 1982), vol. 3, p. 33.

[3] E. B. Pusey, *The Minor Prophets: A Commentary, Zephaniah*, (Grand Rapids: Baker Book House, 1950), vol. 2, p. 245.

[4] John D. Hannah, *The Bible Knowledge Commentary, Zephaniah* (Wheaton: Victor Books, 1985), p. 1528.

CHAPTER 4

[1] Hobart E. Freeman, *An Introduction to the Old Testament Prophets* (Chicago: Moody Press, 1968), p. 104.

[2] E. B. Pusey, *The Minor Prophets: A Commentary, Zephaniah,* (Grand Rapids: Baker Book House, 1953), vol. 2, p. 282.

CHAPTER 5

[1] Cyril J. Barber, *Everyman's Bible Commentary, Habakkuk and Zephaniah* (Chicago: Moody Press, 1985), p. 119.

[2] J. Dwight Pentecost, *Things to Come* (Grand Rapids: Zondervan Publishing House, 1958), p. 519.

[3] Jerry M. Hullinger, *Bibliotheca Sacra: The Problem of Animal Sacrifices in Ezekiel 40-48,* (Dallas: Dallas Theological Seminary, 1995), vol. 152, issue 607, pp. 2-6.

[4] Barber, *op. cit.,* p. 124.

[5] C. F. Keil, *Commentary on the Old Testament, Minor Prophets, Zephaniah,* (Grand Rapids, Wm. B. Eerdmans Publishing Co., 1949), vol. 2, p. 161.

RECOMMENDED READING

Barber, Cyril J. *Everyman's Bible Commentary: Habakkuk and Zephaniah.* Chicago: Moody Press, 1985.

Baxter, J. Sidlow. *Explore the Book: Zephaniah* (6 vols. in 1). Grand Rapids: Zondervan Publishing House, 1970.

Bullock, C. Hassell. *An Introduction to the Old Testament Prophets.* Chicago: Moody Press, 1986.

Feinberg, Charles L. *The Minor Prophets.* Chicago: Moody Press, 1961.

Freeman, Hobart E. *An Introduction to the Old Testament Prophets.* Chicago: Moody Press, 1968.

_____. *Everyman's Bible Commentary: Nahum, Zephaniah, Habakkuk: Minor Prophets of the Seventh Century B.C.* Chicago: Moody Press, 1973.

Hannah, John D. *The Bible Knowledge Commentary: Zephaniah.* Wheaton: Victor Books, 1985.

Ironside, H. A. *Notes on the Minor Prophets.* Neptune, NJ: Loizeaux Brothers, 1909.

Keil, C. F. *Biblical Commentary on the Old Testament: Minor Prophets, Zephaniah*, vol. 2. Grand Rapids: Wm. B. Eerdmans, 1949.

Laetsch, Theo. *The Minor Prophets.* St. Louis: Concordia Publishing House, 1956.

Pusey, E. B. *The Minor Prophets: A Commentary*, vol. 2. Grand Rapids: Baker Book House, 1950.

Tatford, Frederick A. *The Minor Prophets: Prophet of the Watchtower: An Exposition of Habakkuk*, vol. 2. Minneapolis: Klock and Klock Christian Publishers, Inc., 1982.

Unger, Merrill F. *Unger's Commentary on the Old Testament: Zephaniah*, vol. 2. Chicago: Moody Press, 1981.

Walter, Larry Lee. *The Expositor's Bible Commentary: Zephaniah.* Grand Rapids: Zondervan Publishing House, 1985.

PART III

HAGGAI

INTRODUCTION

Haggai's name means *festive* or *festival.* Like a number of the other prophets, no information is provided concerning his family background. Some scholars believe he was born in Judah prior to the Babylonian captivity and saw the glory of Solomon's Temple, but this cannot be proven. He did return with Zerubbabel from captivity and was very old at the time he gave this prophecy. Nothing is known of his occupation other than that he was a prophet, although Jewish tradition teaches that he was a priest. He is mentioned as a prophet in Judah (Ezra 5:1; 6:14-16). Haggai is the second shortest book in the Old Testament and is quoted only once in the New Testament.

The date of Haggai's prophecy is firmly fixed. He wrote in the second year of Darius I (520 B.C.). Haggai assigned a date to each of his four prophecies, all given within four months of each other: August 29, 520 B.C. (1:1); October 17, 520 B.C (2:1); December 18, 520 B.C. (2:10); and again December 18, 520 B.C. (2:20). He directed his prophecy to Zerubbabel the governor, Joshua the high priest (1:1; 2:2, 21), and the people of Judah (1:13).

The setting of Haggai's prophecy is after Judah's return from Babylon (536 B.C.). Babylon was defeated by the Medo-Persian Empire in 536 B.C. The exiles of Judah were under the control of King Cyrus, who allowed them to return to Jerusalem. Back in the land, the Jewish people rebuilt the altar of burnt offering and restored the Temple. However, they refused to allow Samaritan volunteers to have any part in the Temple's reconstruction. The Temple's foundation was laid within two years (Ezra 3:8-10). But the Samaritans were successful in halting work on the Temple through opposition and a direct appeal to the Persian King Cyrus and his son Cambyses. For 16 years, there was no work done on the Temple.

Cambyses succeeded his father Cyrus as King of Persia, but he later committed suicide. Because Cambyses had no son to rule in his place, a number of revolts arose in the Persian Kingdom. Darius I (522-486 B.C.) put down the revolt, and, through his able leadership, peace was restored. Upon finding the original decree of Cyrus, Darius restored it, paving the way for reconstruction of the Temple. In the 16 years that had elapsed, apathy had set in, and the Jewish people showed little interest in completing the Temple. In the second year of Darius (520 B.C.), Haggai began his prophecy, calling on Judah to resume construction of the Temple. It was completed four years later (516 B.C.). This Temple, popularly called Zerubbabel's Temple, began what is known as the Second Temple Period. Zerubbabel's Temple did not possess the beauty of Solomon's Temple or the glory of God and the Ark of the Covenant.

Haggai wrote in a straightforward prose. He used such methods as the curse prophecies of Moses (1:6; cp. Dt. 28:22), rhetorical questions, and terse commands to bring Judah to a place of commitment and service. Haggai's style was effective. Within four weeks of his prophecy, work was begun on the Temple.

Some of the key words in Haggai are *the LORD's house, this house, mine house,* and *consider.* There are two key verses in the book: "And the LORD stirred up the spirit of Zerubbabel, the son of Shealtiel, governor of Judah, and the spirit of Joshua, the son of Jehozadak, the high priest, and the spirit of all the remnant of the people; and they came and did work in the house of the LORD of hosts, their God" (1:14); and "The glory of this latter house shall be greater than of the former, saith the LORD of hosts; and in this place will I give peace, saith the LORD of hosts" (2:9).

Haggai 1:1-15

In the second year of Darius, the king, in the sixth month, in the first day of the month, came the word of the LORD by Haggai, the prophet, unto Zerubbabel, the son of Shealtiel, governor of Judah, and to Joshua, the son of Jehozadak, the high priest, saying, Thus speaketh the LORD of hosts, saying: This people say, The time is not come, the time that the LORD's house should be built. Then came the word of the LORD by Haggai, the prophet, saying, Is it time for you, O ye, to dwell in your paneled houses, and this house to lie waste? Now, therefore, thus saith the LORD of hosts: Consider your ways. Ye have sown much, and bring in little; ye eat, but ye have not enough; ye drink, but ye are not filled with drink; ye clothe yourselves, but there is none warm; and he that earneth wages earneth wages to put it into a bag with holes.

Thus saith the LORD of hosts: Consider your ways. Go up to the mountain, and bring wood, and build the house; and I will take pleasure in it, and I will be glorified, saith the LORD. Ye looked for much and, lo, it came to little; and when ye brought it home, I did blow upon it. Why? saith the LORD of hosts. Because of mine house that is waste, and ye run every man unto his own house. Therefore, the heavens over you withhold the dew, and the earth withholds her fruit. And I called for a drought upon the land, and upon the mountains, and upon the grain, and upon the new wine, and upon the oil, and upon that which the ground bringeth forth, and upon men, and upon cattle, and upon all the labor of the hands.

Then Zerubbabel, the son of Shealtiel, and Joshua, the son of Jehozadak, the high priest, with all the remnant of the people, obeyed the voice of the LORD, their God, and the words of Haggai, the prophet, as the LORD, their God, had sent him, and the people did fear before the LORD. Then spoke Haggai, the LORD's messenger, in the LORD's message unto the people, saying, I am with you, saith the LORD. And the Lord stirred up the spirit of Zerubbabel, the son of Shealtiel, governor of Judah, and the spirit of Joshua, the son of Jehozadak, the high priest, and the spirit of all the remnant of the people; and they came and did work in the house of the LORD of hosts, their God, In the four and twentieth day of the sixth month, in the second year of Darius, the king.

A TIME TO BUILD

America is in the midst of a building boom. Houses are springing up like mushrooms, dotting major expressways and rolling farmland, with price tags unimaginable to past generations. No longer is a house purchased simply for shelter; it is a major luxury investment as a hedge against inflation and taxes.

People spare no expense, time, or effort to provide their families with the right houses in the proper neighborhoods. Families are mortgaged to the hilt for both houses and furnishings in order to have a slice of the American dream. Many people have a second home where they spend the weekends recouping from the mental struggles faced in the corporate world five days a week.

More often than not, Christians find themselves caught up in a similar lifestyle. Drained mentally, physically, and financially by their progressive lifestyles, Christians have little time, interest, or energy for the Lord's work.

Lest you think this characterization is unique to 20th-century Americans, think again. In 502 B.C., the people of Jerusalem were living a materialistic lifestyle with little interest in spiritual things or financial help for God's work.

This is the atmosphere in which Haggai thundered on to the scene with a straightforward prophecy calling the people to renew their commitment and service to God. Failure to do so would bring about complete removal of the little prosperity they had enjoyed upon their return to Jerusalem from Babylonian captivity.

RECIPIENTS OF THE PROPHECY

"In the second year of Darius, the king, in the sixth month, in the first day of the month" (v. 1), or on August 29, 520 B.C., Haggai began to deliver the message God had for Judah.

This date is significant for a number of reasons.

- It provided the exact time of Haggai's prophecy.

- It is taken from the reign of a Persian king, indicating that the "times of the Gentiles" were in progress (Lk. 21:24).

- It was in the sixth month (Elul), indicating that less than one month earlier Judah had remembered the destruction of their Temple by the Babylonians (Av 9, 586 B.C.). The people's hearts were prepared for Haggai's prophecy.

- It was on the first day of the month, a holy day, the time of the new moon, when all work was suspended, as on the Sabbath. A special burnt offering would be presented to the Lord, and the people would listen to the prophets.[1]

Haggai had a captive audience for his captivating prophecy!

The prophet left no doubt that he delivered the message of the Lord and that the people were to respond accordingly (1:1-2, 7, 13; 2:4, 6-9, 11, 14, 23). Before addressing the people, Haggai directed his words to Judah's leadership—Zerubbabel the governor and Joshua the high priest (v. 1).

After Cyrus's decree in 539 B.C., the first group of exiles returned to Judah under Zerubbabel's leadership (Ezra 2:1-2). Zerubbabel was heir to the Davidic throne because he was the grandson of King Jehoiachin (called Jeconiah in 1 Chr. 3:17-19; cp. Mt. 1:12). Thus, Zerubbabel was in the messianic line, a thought picked up by Haggai at the conclusion of his prophecy (2:20-23).

Zerubbabel is called the "son of Shealtiel" (v. 1) and the son of Shealtiel's brother Pedaiah (1 Chr. 3:17-19). This problem is solvable if seen in the light of a levirate marriage (Dt. 25:5-10). Shealtiel took Pedaiah's wife to be his wife after his brother's death; most likely Zerubbabel was then born. *Zerubbabel* means *seed of Babylon*, which is a reference to the country in which he was born. He is referred to as "Sheshbazzar, the prince of Judah" (Ezra 1:8, 11), and the "governor" (Ezra 5:14) of Judah, appointed by Cyrus.

Joshua was the son of Jehozadak (v. 1), the high priest, who was taken into captivity by the Babylonians in 586 B.C. (1 Chr. 6:15).

Haggai presented his message to the political and religious leaders first. If he could ignite their vision to rebuild the Temple, they would inspire the people to finish the task.

REBUKE FOR PROCRASTINATION

Haggai wasted no time in dealing with Judah's excuses for not completing the Temple: "This people say, The time is not come, the time that the LORD's house should be built" (v. 2). The rebuke came from "the LORD of hosts" (LORD of armies, v. 2), a phrase used by the post-exilic prophets to describe an all-powerful God who will accomplish what He has decreed. This was a stern rebuke to a procrastinating people, especially when God would remove any hindrance to enable them to finish the Temple. God did not refer to them as *His* people but as *this* people, showing His displeasure over their disobedience.

Haggai pinpointed the reasons for Judah's procrastination. The people found time to build their own houses, but not God's Temple: "Is it time for you…to dwell in your paneled houses, and this house to lie waste?" (v. 4). The prophet revealed three sins of the people.

1. Their selfishness—they had time and money to construct their own houses, but not God's.

2. The people had become indifferent to the Temple because they had worshiped without it for 70 years in Babylon.

3. Hostile neighbors had disillusioned them from constructing the Temple.

The people were living in "paneled houses" (v. 4), which indicated luxury, "usually associated with royal dwellings such as the palace built by Solomon."[2] Haggai did not specify the type of paneling used, but Zerubbabel purchased cedars from Lebanon to construct the Temple (Ezra 3:7). Could it be that this wood was used to decorate the houses of the wealthy rather than to build the Temple?[3]

God was not rebuking the people for building fine houses for themselves, but for building their own houses while totally neglecting the Lord's house. They were putting self-interest above the Lord's will. How different was the attitude of David. Although he resided in a cedar house, David was totally committed to building a glorious Temple for God (2 Sam. 7:2).

Many Christians worship in buildings inadequate for the congregation or in great need of repair, claiming they lack the funds to upgrade the church building. Yet these congregants spare no expense in beautifying or upgrading their own houses, along with securing all of the creature comforts available. Like Judah, many Christians are unaware that their actions have cut short the blessings God has for them.

REASON FOR POVERTY

Haggai awakened Judah to their plight with the words, "Consider your ways" (v. 5), or *Set your heart upon your way* (cp. 1:7; 2:15, 18). The prophet was saying, *Give very careful thought in reflecting on your priorities. Make the proper adjustments and follow the Lord's will.*

Haggai reviewed the material blessings God had removed because of the nation's disobedience.

1. Their agriculture failed: "Ye have sown much, and bring in little" (v. 6). Although they planted much seed, the harvest was a disaster (cp. 1:10-11; 2:15-17).

2. The economy of the land was not sufficient to meet the people's needs: "ye eat, but ye have not enough; ye drink, but ye are not filled with drink: ye clothe yourselves, but there is none warm" (v. 6).

3. Inflation was spiraling out of control because of famine and the scarcity of goods: "and he that earneth wages earneth wages to put it into a bag with holes" (v. 6). There was not enough money to meet the needs of daily life. We are reminded of the bumper sticker that says, "My take-home pay will not take me home."

This chastening was direct from God because of their disobedience. Moses had predicted these very judgments centuries earlier (Lev. 26:18-20; Dt. 28:38-40). The secret to Judah's personal blessing depended on their obedience to God—putting the Temple construction before their own welfare. Christ spoke to this very issue when he said, "But seek ye first the kingdom of God, and his righteousness, and all these things shall be added unto you" (Mt. 6:33).

REBUILDING PROMOTED

Once again, Haggai called Judah to consider their ways (v. 7) and gather more timber to build the Temple (v. 8). They were to repent of their sins and get on with the renewed task of reconstructing the Temple. In so doing, God would take pleasure in the Temple and be glorified or honored through its completion (v. 8). This in turn would be a sign to the surrounding nations that God had restored Judah to its previous state, and it was now in a position to receive His blessing.

REVIEWING THEIR PLIGHT

If Judah refused to build the Temple, it would mean a total collapse of its economic system. The people might plant an abundance of seed with great hope of a plenteous harvest, but little would be produced, and even that would be blown away by God (v. 9). Why? God said, "Because of mine house that is waste, and ye run every man unto his own house" (v. 9). The people were constructing their own houses but had no time for or interest in working on God's Temple. Thus, the Lord would remove all of their prosperity as a judgment upon them.

The same is true today. Christians find time in their busy schedules to spend hours constructing new houses—whether it be time spent choosing the right lots, making sure the blueprints are drawn properly, picking out paint, carpet, and fixtures, or watching the buildings go up to make certain nothing is done wrong. But when it comes to building the church, the opposite is often true. The cheapest materials are used, and the lowest bidder is contracted for the work. When members are asked to help with inside finishing work, few respond, and those who do give little time to the project.

God intervened directly in the affairs of Judah to cause an economic disaster. Tremendous drought set in when He withheld "the dew" (v. 10). Heavy dew is needed in Israel, especially in the dry season, to produce a bountiful summer crop. The drought affected everything—the grain (barley and wheat), new wine, and oil (olive oil used in food, medicine, and ointments) [v. 11]. Such crop failures would devastate humans and animals alike, depriving them of the needed sustenance to live. People laboring in the fields toiled in vain because their efforts would come to naught (v. 11).

Although most Americans do not acquire their livelihoods through farming, God has used other methods to cause economic disaster. The stock market has taken several huge plunges in recent years, sweeping away the fortunes of many. Such plunges shock the corporate world into seeing how vulnerable it is to quick economic disaster. Could it be that God is starting to shake the economic foundation of America because of its gross materialism and spiritual callousness? Remember, no nation, state, or individual is exempt from such disaster when refusing to heed God's warning.

RENEWAL OF THE PROJECT

Judah's response was immediate. They "obeyed the voice of the LORD...and the words of Haggai...and the people did fear before the LORD" (v. 12). Lest we think it was easy for Judah to make such an about-face, remember that they had been disobedient for 16 years. Such a self-serving lifestyle would be hard to turn away from, but when the piercing Word of God penetrated their hearts, change took place immediately.

Upon witnessing Judah's repentance, renewal, and reverential respect for the Lord, the tone of Haggai's message changed from judgment to comfort. God's comforting word was short and encouraging: "I am with you" (v. 13). Need anymore be said? This was divine assurance that God would empower, protect, guide, and accomplish His task through the people. Such a word of encouragement should drive out all fear of the enemy and fortify the people to finish what God required.

The Lord's "I am with you" has encouraged God's people through the centuries:

- Isaac and Jacob (Gen. 26:3; 28:15)

- Moses in delivering Israel (Ex. 4:12)

- Joshua leading Israel to Canaan (Josh. 1:5)

- Jeremiah at his call (Jer. 1:8)

- Israel during times of tribulation (Isa. 43:1)

- The disciples at their commission (Mt. 28:19-20)

- Paul in going to Corinth (Acts 18:10)

If God was with these men of old, will He be with Christians today? Of course He will! He has promised to be with all those who are obedient to His voice (Rom. 8:31; Heb. 13:5). Christians must grasp God's "I am with you" and act accordingly.

Haggai's prophecy "stirred up the spirit of Zerubbabel...Joshua... and...the people; and they came and did work in the house of the LORD" (v. 14). First, the leadership was stirred from indifference to obey God's voice. A people can only rise as high as the leadership is willing to take them.

Second, they were not just stirred for the moment; they were stirred to build the Temple. Paul told Timothy to "stir up the gift of God" that had been bestowed on him (2 Tim. 1:6). Christians have a responsibility to continually stir themselves and use their God-given gifts for His glory.

Third, "they came and did work" (v. 14). There was no more murmuring or complaining that they could not afford to build, that it was not time to build, or that they did not need the Temple. They were ready and eager to get on with the God-given task of constructing the Temple. The same should be true in the church, but all too often Christians shrink from being stirred to the work because of timidity, a sense of inability, lack of faith, recession, or just plain apathy.

On September 21, 520 B.C., just 23 days later, work was begun on the Temple. Judah had responded to Haggai's message, but it took three weeks to plan the work and prepare the materials for construction—a very short time, considering that the project had lain dormant for 16 years. When God calls, there is to be prompt obedience, even though there may be intervening time before people actually begin His work.

Like Judah, many Christians should take a spiritual inventory of themselves and ask some very penetrating questions.

- Has my spiritual vision been dimmed by materialistic pursuits?

- Has commitment to my profession consumed both time and energy, so that there is none left for the Lord's service?

- Am I so caught in the web of financial debt that my giving to the Lord's work is, at best, insufficient or almost nonexistent?

Judah had to rethink its priorities and draw a new blueprint for its spiritual life. Some of us should do likewise. It is time to build. Build a life that will please God!

Haggai 2:1-9

In the seventh month, in the one and twentieth day of the month, came the word of the LORD by the prophet Haggai, saying, Speak now to Zerubbabel, the son of Shealtiel, governor of Judah, and to Joshua, the son of Jehozadak, the high priest, and to the residue of the people, saying, Who is left among you that saw this house in its first glory? And how do ye see it now? Is it not in your eyes in comparison with it as nothing? Yet now be strong, O Zerubbabel, saith the LORD; and be strong, O Joshua, son of Jehozadak, the high priest; and be strong, all ye people of the land, saith the LORD, and work; for I am with you, saith the LORD of hosts. According to the word that I covenanted with you when ye came out of Egypt, so my Spirit remaineth among you; fear not. For thus saith the LORD of hosts: Yet once, it is a little while, and I will shake the heavens, and the earth, and the sea, and the dry land; And I will shake all nations, and the desire of all nations shall come; and I will fill this house with glory, saith the LORD of hosts. The silver is mine, and the gold is mine, saith the LORD of hosts. The glory of this latter house shall be greater than of the former, saith the LORD of hosts; and in this place will I give peace, saith the LORD of hosts.

A TIME TO ENCOURAGE

Haggai's message had stirred Judah from idleness. The sound of workmen removing 60 years of rubble, refacing stones, and beginning to build on the foundation laid 16 years earlier filled Jerusalem. But less than a month after the work had begun, it was interrupted by three religious feasts on Israel's calendar. In the seventh month, the month of Tishri (September-October), the Feast of Trumpets was on the first day, the Day of Atonement on the tenth day, and the Feast of Tabernacles from the 15th day through the 21st day.

Knowing that such delays could dampen the people's enthusiastic drive to complete the task, Haggai stepped forward with a message of encouragement from the Lord. He delivered his second message in the "seventh month, in the one and twentieth day of the month" (v. 1), the final day of the Feast of Tabernacles, which fell on October 17, 520 B.C.

The Feast of Tabernacles (Booths) (Lev. 23:34-44) is also called the Feast of Ingathering and is the final religious celebration on Israel's annual calendar. It commemorated the end of the fall harvest, the ingathering of crops, and the remembrance of God's protection during Israel's 40 years in the wilderness, when the people lived in tents.

A number of rituals accompanied this seven-day feast. For seven days the people lived in booths constructed of palm, willow, and leaf tree branches and decorated with fruit.

There was the daily procession to the Gihon Spring, where the priest filled a golden pitcher with water, returned to the Temple, and poured it on the altar. This was done as a reminder of God's supernatural provision of water for Israel during their 40 years in the wilderness.

The feast ended with all the people gathered in Jerusalem for a religious festival. This would not have been a joyful festival in 520 B.C., for drought had destroyed their crops, and the Temple was not completed—a grim reminder of the destruction they had suffered during the Babylonian invasion. The prophet's message of encouragement was like water to a thirsty soul for people who were weary and discouraged.

COMPARING THE TEMPLES

Great hope filled the elders of Judah, who envisioned a Temple possessing the glories they had gazed upon before their captivity. But as the walls went up, the people's spirits came down, for Zerubbabel's Temple paled in splendor to King Solomon's.

Knowing that discouragement was beginning to set in, Haggai asked three rhetorical questions that would reveal the people's true attitude toward the Temple they were constructing. First he asked, "Who is left among you that saw this house in its first glory?" (v. 3).

Many had witnessed the beauty of Solomon's Temple, which had been destroyed 66 years earlier—possibly Haggai was one of them. The glory of Solomon's Temple was something to behold. It was twice the size of the Tabernacle: 90 feet long, 30 feet wide, and 45 feet high. It was strikingly beautiful in appearance because of its white limestone, cedar, and gold exterior. The entire interior of the Temple was covered with cedar (walls) and pine (floor) boards, all overlaid with gold. The holy place was 60 feet long, decorated with carved gourds, cherubim, palm trees, and open flowers. The altar of incense was made of cedar overlaid with gold. Gold chains were hung in the holy place across the doors that led into the holy of holies. The holy place contained ten golden lampstands and ten golden tables of showbread.

The holy of holies was a 30-foot cube, all overlaid with gold. Two gigantic cherubim, made of olive wood and covered with gold, extended the length of the room with their outstretched wings touching at the tips. The walls of the Temple were decorated with carved cherubim, palm trees, and open flowers. All of the doors were decorated like the walls.[1] Years ago, it was estimated that more than $20,000,000 worth of gold was used just to cover the holy of holies.[2]

One writer stated, "The Babylonian Talmud indicated that Zerubbabel's Temple lacked five glories that were present in Solomon's Temple:

1. the ark of the covenant;

2. the holy fire;

3. the Shekinah glory;

4. the Spirit of prophecy (the Holy Spirit);

5. the Urim and Thummim."[3]

The answer to the second question, "And how do ye see it now?" (v. 3), was self-evident. Obviously they considered it inferior to Solomon's Temple.

The third question provided the answer: "Is it not in your eyes in comparison with it as nothing?" (v. 3). The expected answer is, *Yes!* Response to the completed Temple would have been similar to the response at the dedication of the foundation. Those who had not seen the glory of Solomon's Temple would have praised the Lord; but the older generation, those who had lived before the Temple's destruction, wept loudly and profusely because Zerubbabel's Temple was nothing in comparison to Solomon's.

COURAGE FOR THE TASK

Haggai encouraged the people to finish the project, telling them to "be strong" (v. 4), or *take courage.* The people needed encouragement to complete the task, for they feared opposition like that which arose during the laying of the foundation.

Sixteen years earlier, opposition had arisen from Tatnai and Shethar-bozenai (Ezra 5:3), who questioned Judah's right to commence the reconstruction of the Temple. Tatnai had written to King Darius, opposing the construction (Ezra 5:16-17). Darius searched the archives for documentation of Judah's right to build. A scroll was found confirming that right, and Darius ordered the Temple to be completed, warning Tatnai not to interfere with the work (Ezra 6:1-12). Obviously this opposition had ceased because Haggai made no mention of it.

The words "be strong" were followed by the command "and work" (v. 4). David had encouraged Solomon in like manner when he committed the original Temple project to him (1 Chr. 28:10, 20). Any project so massive would require strength and courage.

When the torch of leadership was passed from Moses to Joshua,

God gave the same encouraging word to him. Three times God commanded Joshua to "be strong and of good courage" (Josh. 1:6-7, 9). He was to be strong and courageous because of God's promise: "for unto this people shalt thou divide for an inheritance the land which I swore unto their fathers" (Josh. 1:6). He was to be strong and courageous in obeying God's law by meditating on the Word of God and manifesting it through his life. In so doing, the Lord would prosper him (Josh. 1:7). He was to be strong and courageous because God's presence would go with him (Josh. 1:9) to provide victory over Israel's enemies.

In like manner, Judah was to be strong and courageous in building the Temple, for God promised to help them finish the task, as He had Joshua. God took pleasure in the Temple's completion because it would glorify Him (1:8). As He had with Joshua, God promised to prosper Judah if they obeyed His Word by completing the Temple. As God had promised that His presence would be with Joshua, so He would be with Judah as they worked on the Temple, for God said, "I am with you" (v. 4). God has promised to be with all those who follow the *faith formula* given to Joshua.

Judah was to trust the Lord for two reasons. First, God promised to be with them just as He had covenanted when delivering them from their Egyptian slavery (v. 5). He had covenanted to shepherd them during their 40 years in the wilderness and to give them the land of Canaan as well. Second, as the Spirit of God was with them coming out of Egypt, so He would remain among them in building the Temple. Therefore, the words "fear not" (v. 5) undergirded them with the needed confidence to finish the Temple's construction.

Christians who are indwelt by the Holy Spirit and yielded to His direction can be assured of God's presence and power to undertake any task they have been called to perform.

CREATION TREMBLES

God said, in "a little while...I will shake the heavens, and the earth, and the sea, and the dry land; And...all nations" (vv. 6-7a). The words *a little while* are not speaking of an *immediate* shaking but an *imminent* shaking of the earth, meaning that it could happen at any time.

Just when will this shaking take place? Some commentators tie the shaking to verse 5 and say that it refers to God's power in delivering Israel from Egypt through the Red Sea and the manifestation of His power before the Israelites when Mount Sinai quaked. Others see the phrase as referring to God's stirring of Darius (Ezra 6:6-15) to supply help and gifts to Ezra so that Judah could build the Temple. Still others believe that the shaking refers to God's bringing future judgment upon the Persians, Greeks, and Romans. But the context of this passage is futuristic and refers to the Messiah's Second Coming, when God will "shake the heavens and earth" (2:21; Joel 3:16; Zech. 14:4-5; Mt. 24:29; Rev. 16:18, 20) and destroy Gentile world rule (2:22; Dan. 2:34-35, 44-45). The writer of Hebrews interpreted Haggai 2:6 in the context of God's shaking the earth and nations at the Second Coming of Christ (Heb. 12:26-27). He went on to say that after the Millennial Kingdom, God will again shake the heavens and the earth, which will bring about the total destruction of the universe (2 Pet. 3:10, 12; Rev. 20:11). Then a new heaven and a new earth will appear (2 Pet. 3:13; Rev. 21:1).

Added to the difficulty of this section is the precise interpretation of the phrase, "the desire of all nations shall come" (v. 7). The word *desire* has been translated personally referring to the Messiah and impersonally referring to desirable things (i.e., treasure, wealth). Controversy over the correct interpretation has revolved around the use of a plural verb, *come*, with a singular noun, *desire*. Even after a thorough study of the grammatical problem, there is no conclusive interpretation agreed upon by scholars. Because verse 8 refers to silver and gold, most modern scholars believe that *desire* refers to the nations bringing their wealth to the Millennial Temple.

Herbert Wolf may have had the true interpretation when he wrote, "Ultimately it does apply to the gathering of the treasures of nations after the Second Coming of Christ...but it can also refer to the 'treasure' or 'desire of nations' "[4]—that is, the Messiah. He is the only one who could fulfill their desire for peace on earth (2:9).

Haggai went on to reveal that God would "fill this house with glory" (v. 7), and "The glory of this latter house shall be greater than of the former" (v. 9). The prophet was contrasting the two *glories* of the two Temples.

How should the word *glory* be interpreted? Does it refer to the material beauty of the Temple or to God's presence in the Temple? Both can be seen because verse 8 refers to the material glory and verse 9 mentions God's glory, but the thrust of the passage refers to God's glory in the Temple.

Haggai was saying that the glory of Zerubbabel's Temple would be greater than that of Solomon's. But how could this be, inasmuch as Zerubbabel's Temple did not possess the material glory or the Shekinah glory? First, God viewed the various Temples constructed throughout Israel's history as one continuous Temple. Herod's Temple was not considered another Temple but a continuation of Zerubbabel's.

Second, glory came to Herod's Temple in the person of Christ at His dedication (Lk. 2:21-24). He was greater than the Temple (Mt. 12:6), greater than Solomon (Mt. 12:42), and His glory will one day fill the Millennial Temple (Rev. 21:22-23).

Third, God said, "in this place [Jerusalem and the Temple] will I give peace" (v. 9). This peace will come to fruition when Christ,

"The Prince of Peace" (Isa. 9:6), comes to establish it at His Second Coming. At that time, peace will flow like a river from Jerusalem to the whole world (Isa. 66:12).

Judah was to realize that although Zerubbabel's Temple did not possess the material beauty of Solomon's Temple, their work was of great importance. It forged a link between Temples in which the Messiah's glory and peace would ultimately be manifested in the Kingdom age. Therefore, the people were to do their work heartily as unto the Lord.

Like Haggai, Jesus used the Feast of Tabernacles to deliver a stirring revelation of comfort and encouragement to Judah. John wrote, "In the last day, that great day of the feast, Jesus stood and cried out, saying, If any man thirst, let him come unto me, and drink. He that believeth on me, as the scripture hath said, out of his heart shall flow rivers of living water" (Jn. 7:37-38). He was saying, *I am the one who provides the water of salvation to all who thirst. Those who come and drink* (believe in Christ) *will be given eternal life, and out of their hearts will flow rivers of living water.* The ministry of the Holy Spirit would be a source of strength, guidance, power, and peace in the lives of believers.

Christians are working on a "Temple" for God's glory, but it is not made of stone and cedar. The church body is the Temple of the Holy Spirit in which God's glory resides (1 Cor. 6:19). For God's glory to be manifested through the body:

1. All of the rubble of sin must be removed (1 Cor. 6:15-20).

2. Each stone (Christian) within the fellowship must be continually shaped into Christ's image (Rom. 8:29).

3. The building constructed of gold, silver, and precious stones must be properly laid on the foundation of Christ (1 Cor. 3:11-12).

What type of builder are you? Are you a shoddy builder, using inferior materials, careless and inept in your service for Christ, causing discouragement within the church? God wants us to be master builders, constructing with good materials, careful in our service, which will greatly encourage others and glorify God.

Haggai 2:10-23

In the four and twentieth day of the ninth month, in the second year of Darius, came the word of the LORD by Haggai, the prophet, saying, Thus saith the LORD of hosts: Ask now the priests concerning the law, saying, If one bear holy flesh in the skirt of his garment, and with his skirt do touch bread, or pottage, or wine, or oil, or any food, shall it be holy? And the priests answered and said, No. Then said Haggai, If one that is unclean by a dead body touch any of these, shall it be unclean? And the priests answered and said, It shall be unclean. Then answered Haggai, and said, So is this people, and so is this nation before me, saith the LORD; and so is every work of their hands; and that which they offer there is unclean. And now, I pray you, consider from this day and upward, from before a stone was laid upon a stone in the temple of the LORD; Since those days were, when one came to an heap of twenty measures, there were but ten; when one came to the winevat to draw out fifty vessels out of the press, there were but twenty. I smote you with blight and with mildew and with hail in all the labors of your hands; yet ye turned not to me, saith the LORD. Consider now from this day and upward, from the four and twentieth day of the ninth month, even from the day that the foundation of the LORD's temple was laid, consider it. Is the seed yet in the barn? Yea, as yet the vine, and the fig tree, and the pomegranate, and the olive tree, have not brought forth; from this day will I bless you.

And again the word of the LORD came unto Haggai in the four and twentieth day of the month, saying, Speak to Zerubbabel, governor of Judah, saying, I will shake the heavens and the earth; And I will overthrow the throne of kingdoms, and I will destroy the strength of the kingdoms of the nations; and I will overthrow the chariots, and those who ride in them; and the horses and their riders shall come down, every one by the sword of his brother. In that day, saith the LORD of hosts, will I take thee, O Zerubbabel, my servant, the son of Shealtiel, saith the LORD, and will make thee as a signet; for I have chosen thee, saith the LORD of hosts.

A TIME FOR RENEWAL

The summer of 1988 will be remembered for the drought that affected much of the country. Relentless heat and rainless days wilted crops and wasted livestock. As a result, many farmers declared bankruptcy and waited for the auctioneer to liquidate their properties. Without grain, the herdsmen had to slaughter their livestock earlier than expected, in some cases destroying genetically developed breeds that will take years to replace.

In the biblical account, Judah had been suffering a similar drought, but, in its case, it was a definite chastening from the Lord. In his third message, Haggai reminded the sinful nation that God's chastening hand would be lifted only if the people turned to God for cleansing and completed the Temple's construction.

CLEANSING BEFORE RENEWAL

The Prophet Haggai delivered his third message on "the four and twentieth day of the ninth month, in the second year of Darius" (v. 10)—December 18, 520 B.C.

Haggai asked the priests two questions concerning ceremonial cleansing. First, he requested a ruling on the matter of ritual: "If one bear holy flesh in the skirt of his garment, and with his skirt do touch bread, or pottage, or wine, or oil, or any food, shall it be holy?" (v. 12). The "holy flesh" was that portion set aside to be sacrificed to the Lord. Often, a priest carried the flesh for the sacrifice in his robe, which meant that his garment became holy (Lev. 6:27). Therefore, Haggai questioned, if the holy flesh touched other food items, was holiness transferred to them as well? The priests answered, "No," for holiness cannot be transferred to items of food.

Haggai asked a second question of the priests, this one dealing with the transfer of ritual defilement. "If one that is unclean by a dead body touch any of these, shall it be unclean?" (v. 13). The priests answered, *Yes, the Israelite would become ritually defiled* (v. 13; cp. Lev. 11:28; 22:4-7). The Mosaic Law taught that moral cleanness cannot be transmitted, but moral uncleanness can. The same is true in the physical life. Health between people cannot be transferred, but sickness can.

Haggai applied the official answer from the priests to the people's condition: "So is this people, and so is this nation...and so is every work of their hands" (v. 14). The application is clear: Israel had originally been holy and set apart for the Lord's use (Ex. 19:6), but the nation now was defiled, and everything it touched became unclean.

Once again God referred to Judah, not as *my* people, but as *this* people and *this* nation (v. 14), showing His displeasure over their walk before Him. God expressed His displeasure because of Judah's disobedience (1:2-4). The nation had failed to do His will in completing the Temple.

Disobedience made Judah ceremonially unclean, which meant that any sacrifice or form of service was unacceptable to the Lord (v. 14). Therefore, divine blessing had been withheld from the people, individually and nationally.

There is a growing sense that many Christian workers are serving God with unclean hearts and hands. They live as if God has winked at their sin, and because they are working for the Lord He will continue to bless them. Blessing may come to an individual or his or her organization for a season, but it comes more because of a praying spouse, family, or committed followers. Eventually a person's ungodliness is revealed, the Lord's discipline ensues, and judgment falls. God is not deceived, nor will He be mocked by unclean servants, "for whatever a man soweth, that shall he also reap" (Gal. 6:7). Sadly, leaders not only pull themselves down by their actions, but the lives and testimonies of many innocent people are tarnished or permanently damaged.

Today it appears that a number of Christian leaders have capitalized on their sin and fall. True, it seems that they are humiliated by their experiences, but after repentance, counseling, and a few months of rehabilitation, they return to the Lord's service. Often Christendom provides them even greater exposure for ministry, as well as opportunities to gain financial profit from books written about their experiences.

CALL TO RENEWAL

With bluntness in his first message, the prophet called the nation of Judah to renewal (1:5, 7), but in chapter 2, verse 15, he tenderly entreated the nation: "And now, I pray you, consider from this day and upward" (v. 15). The phrase "this day and upward" (vv.

15, 18) pointed in two directions. First, the nation was to reflect back 16 years, "before a stone was laid...in the temple of the LORD" (vv. 15, 18). During those years, the people did not receive blessings from the Lord because of their uncleanness (v. 14). The wheat crop, which should have produced "twenty measures" at harvest, yielded only ten measures (v. 16), a loss of 50 percent. They had hoped to glean 50 vessels of wine from their vineyards, but production came to only 20 vessels (v. 16), a loss of 60 percent (cp. 1:6-11).

It was now the ninth month, and Haggai asked the nation, "Is the seed yet in the barn?" (v. 19). Seed had been harvested between April and September, but drought had so severely impacted the yield that there was little to gather. The obvious answer was, *No, the harvest is not in the barn!*

Although the people had turned to the Lord on September 21, 520 B.C. (1:14), the effects of God's past judgment were still being felt. He had smitten the land with "blight [scorching wind] and with mildew and with hail" (v. 17). This past judgment had not produced national repentance, for the Lord said, "yet ye turned not to me" (v. 17).

Haggai echoed the same message proclaimed by Amos. He predicted that the Lord would chasten Israel with famine, drought, blight, locust, plagues, military defeat, and devastation (Amos 4:6-11). Five times Amos declared, "yet have ye not returned unto me, saith the LORD" (Amos 4:6, 8-11). Because of their rebellion, Israel was to "prepare to meet...God" (Amos 4:12)—that is, be ready for coming judgment.

During the 1988 drought and since, many climatologists believed that the nation was experiencing what is called the *greenhouse effect.* When fossil fuels are burned, they emit carbon dioxide, which acts as a blanket, trapping heat in the atmosphere. This produces a rise in the earth's temperature, causing warmer, drier summers. Climatologists go on to say that this trend will grow worse unless the use of fossil fuels is curtailed. The drought experienced in 1988 and others in recent years may have been warnings from God that judgment is coming unless the nation returns to the Lord.

Twice in this section, Judah is called to "consider" its way (vv. 15, 18). It was to reflect on 16 years of disobedience and judgment and turn from sin to the Lord, so that He could bring blessing.

Second, Judah was to consider "this day and upward" (vv. 15, 18). Because the nation had repented of its sin and responded to the prophet's message, it was to mark December 18, 520 B.C., as a watershed between past judgment and future blessing. The phrase "from this day will I bless you" (v. 19) was an encouraging word from the prophet. "This day" marked a turning point in Judah's history.

Life is full of turning points for Christians. Often they stand at a fork on life's road, needing to make decisions that will affect themselves and those around them. If they make decisions that are self-serving and outside of God's will, their lives will be full of weariness and waste for years to come. But by walking down the path of righteousness, believers find the way of blessing. The key is found in Jesus' words, "But seek ye first the kingdom of God, and his righteousness, and all these things shall be added unto you" (Mt. 6:33). The word *seek* is a present tense imperative meaning to *continually seek* God's Kingdom and righteousness. Believers are to possess a constant hunger and thirst for holiness and the spiritual things of God's Kingdom, not the material things of life. When believers live that kind of life, they need not worry about material things. God has promised to provide them.

CONQUEST AFTER RENEWAL

Haggai proclaimed his final message to Zerubbabel again on the 24th day of the ninth month—December 18, 520 B.C. (v. 20). He announced that Israel's enemies would be judged, and the long-expected Messianic blessing would come to the nation.

KINGDOMS SHAKEN

The prophet revealed that God would "shake the heavens and the earth; And...overthrow the throne of kingdoms" (vv. 21-22). This shaking (earthquake) will be a divine judgment poured out on the nations during the Tribulation. The judgment will be total. Nations will suffer a catastrophic "overthrow" (v. 22) like that of Sodom and Gomorrah. The chariots (v. 22) or war machinery of these nations will be destroyed like those of Egypt in the Red Sea (Ex. 14:28). The nations will become confused in battle and destroy themselves, "every one by the sword of his brother" (v. 22), as in the day when Gideon defeated the Midianites (Jud. 7:22). This prophecy will be fulfilled during the Tribulation.

KING SELECTED

Haggai revealed, "In that day, saith the LORD of hosts, will I take thee, O Zerubbabel, my servant...and will make thee as a signet" (v. 23). The prophet did not say *this* day but *that* day, connecting this prophecy with future events. But how can this prophecy refer to Zerubbabel, who would have died centuries before its fulfillment?

It must be noted that in this passage, Zerubbabel is not called "governor," as he previously was (1:1, 14; 2:2, 21), but "my servant." The phrase *my servant* is a title used in reference to David (Isa. 37:35), Israel as a nation (Isa. 41:8-16; 44:1-8, 21; 45:4; 48:20), and the Messiah (Isa. 42:1-12; 49; 52:13-15; 53:1-12). Because Zerubbabel was in the line of David and the line of the Messiah (Mt. 1:12-13), the passage is to be taken symbolically, like that of Joshua's crowning as high priest (Zech. 3:1-10). The emphasis in this verse is on position, not personal fulfillment. When the Messiah comes at the end of the Great Tribulation, He will be from the line of Zerubbabel and will take His seat on David's throne to rule forever (Lk. 1:32-33).

King's Signet

Zerubbabel was to be made "as a signet" ring (v. 23) before the nation of Judah. The signet was used in three ways:

1. As a person's signature.

2. To validate royal authority within the document sealed (1 Ki. 21:8).

3. As a guarantee to fulfill a future promise (Gen. 38:18).

The signet always represented the owner. In biblical times, it was worn on the right hand (Jer. 22:24) or hung around the neck.[1]

How did the signet apply to Zerubbabel? The answer is found in a prophecy in Jeremiah 22:24-25 concerning Zerubbabel's ancestry. Before the Babylonian captivity, God told Coniah (Jeconiah), Zerubbabel's grandfather, that although he was a signet upon His right hand, he would be plucked off His hand and given to Nebuchadnezzar. This prophecy was fulfilled in 597 B.C. when the king was carried off to Babylon by Nebuchadnezzar.

It was prophesied of Coniah, "Write this man childless, a man that shall not prosper in his days; for no man of his seed shall prosper, sitting upon the throne of David, and ruling any more in Judah" (Jer. 22:30). This did not mean that the king would be childless, for he was not (1 Chr. 3:17-18; Mt. 1:12), but that he was *written* childless—that is, none of his descendants would be listed with the kings of Judah.

Some may ask, *Wasn't Joseph, Jesus' father, from the line of Jeconiah* (Mt. 1:12, 16), *disqualifying Jesus from the right to occupy the throne of David?* Yes, Joseph was the father of Jesus, but he was not His

physical father. Christ's right to the throne of David came physically through Mary, whose genealogy is traced to David through
Nathan, not through Solomon (Lk. 3:31; Mt. 1:17). Thus, Jesus
has the legal right to sit on David's throne and rule.

When Zerubbabel became God's signet, the curse of judgment
was reversed, and the Lord assured the governor that blessing would
once more flow to Judah. This was symbolic of the blessing yet to
come on Judah during the Messiah's reign.

There is an interesting play on words with the name *Zerubbabel*,
which means *seed of Babylon*. It was the seed of Coniah who was
cast into the land of Babylon and would not prosper (Jer. 22:28-30),
but during the return to Judah, the seed of Coniah (Zerubbabel)
would lead the people from Babylon. Zerubbabel represented the
Messiah, who would ultimately deliver Israel from bondage, rebuild
the Temple, and restore physical and spiritual blessing to the land.

Haggai ended his prophecy with the words, "saith the LORD of
hosts" (v. 23). The name *LORD of Hosts* (*Jehovah Sabaoth*) is mentioned 14 times in the Book of Haggai. The name portrays God as
an all-powerful King, a mighty warrior who defends His people
against their enemies. During the Kingdom age, He will manifest
His universal reign from Israel in total authority and Lordship.

Today the Lord sovereignly reigns in the affairs of mankind.
Such things as droughts are not quirks of history, the happenstance
of changing weather patterns, or tricks of mother nature. They are
direct warnings of possible judgment from God.

Judah's lack of prosperity was in direct relation to its spiritual
condition; thus it needed spiritual renewal before the refreshing
rains would revitalize the land. So it is with the United States.
Instead of churches calling, "Come, pray with us for rain," as they
did during the 1988 drought, the cry should have been, "Come,
pray with us for spiritual renewal."

Like Judah, the social, political, and religious evils in this country have marked out the nation for judgment. The cup of America's sin is rapidly being filled to the brim and is about to overflow. Like the prophets of old, many Christian leaders have stepped forward to voice their concerns about our sick society. And, like Habakkuk, they are voices trying to stem the tide of moral decay eating away at the fabric of our nation. Their message echoes through the corridors of our country. Ominous clouds of God's judgment are beginning to hover on the horizon, and their shadow is a warning that judgment may not be far off.

In his book, *The Culting of America*, Ron Rhodes profiles disturbing trends in America, already mentioned in this volume, that could well bring God's judgment upon this nation.[2] They are:

1. The rejection of absolute truth.

2. A majority of Americans embracing moral relativism.

3. A growing proportion of Americans (one-third of the population) not believing in the God of the Bible.

4. The belief that it does not matter what god you pray to because the deities of the world religions are ultimately the same deity, yet shrouded in different names and attributes by all faiths.

5. Nearly two out of three American adults contending that the choice of one religious faith over another is irrelevant because all faiths teach the same basic lessons about life.

6. A large number of impotent and lifeless Christian churches producing indifference, lack of commitment, spiritual dryness, doctrinal immaturity, and biblical illiteracy among members.

7. The rise of cultic and occult groups, along with Eastern religions, penetrating every area of American culture.

8. The pervasive disillusionment coupled with a lack of direction among America's youth.

9. The perverted emphasis and use of money, sexual perversion and promiscuity, violence, and power.

10. The family structure shifting from couples to single-parent and same-sex-marriage households, which provide little or no religious foundation for their children.

Many people in this country believe that America is different from other nations and will somehow escape the tragic decline and ultimate destruction suffered by past civilizations. Such is not the case. A study of world history indicates that the average age of a nation ranges between 200 and 250 years. In his article, "The Decline of a Nation," Kerby Anderson states,

> Each of the great civilizations of the world passed through a series of stages from their birth to their decline to their death. Historians have listed these in ten stages. The first stage moves from bondage to spiritual faith. The second stage moves from spiritual faith to great courage. The third stage moves from great courage to liberty. The fourth stage moves from liberty to abundance. The fifth stage moves from abundance to selfishness. The sixth stage moves from selfishness to complacency. The seventh stage moves from complacency to apathy. The eighth stage moves from apathy to moral decay. The ninth stage moves from moral decay to dependence. And the tenth and last stage moves from dependence to bondage....The book of Judges shows that the nation of Israel passed through these

same stages. And this country will do the same
unless revival and reformation break out and reverse
the inexorable decline of this nation.[3]

Attitudes are divided in America. Some Americans are putting
their houses in order, sensing that God's wrath could fall upon this
country at any moment and sweep away the freedoms and prosperity enjoyed for the past two centuries. Others are apathetic about it
all, enjoying the good life, eating, drinking, and being merry—
unaware of the awesome disaster awaiting America.

When prophetic voices warn of coming judgment, the only
hope for a nation is spiritual renewal. But for spiritual renewal to
be national, it must first be individual—each one of us is the key.
A simple formula for revival was given to Solomon at the dedication of Judah's first Temple. In his prayer of dedication, Solomon
requested help for Judah when it sinned individually and nationally against God (2 Chr. 6:22-40). Twelve years later, God
appeared to Solomon a second time and gave His formula for the
spiritual healing of the nation. God said to Solomon, "If my people, who are called by my name, shall humble themselves, and
pray, and seek my face, and turn from their wicked ways, then will
I hear from heaven, and will forgive their sin, and will heal their
land" (2 Chr. 7:14).

First, renewal depends on *relationship*—not between God and
the political leadership, or education, or urban renewal, or social
rehabilitation, but between God and His people. God said, "If
my people, who are called by my name," will take the initiative
to seek Me, then restoration can occur. This is not some quick-
fix, a few minutes spent in prayer requesting God to stay His
hand of judgment. It takes quality time spent in prayer and personal meditation, beseeching God for the winds of revival to
sweep over America.

Second, restoration depends on three *requirements* of God's people when they come before Him.

1. They must "humble themselves"—that is, come before God without pride or pretense, in a spirit of meekness and lowliness, when praying for their nation. They must be like Nehemiah (Neh. 1:6), who humbled himself before God, acknowledging individual and national sins, earnestly pleading in prayer for his nation.

2. They must "seek my face," says the Lord. To seek God's face is to desire His personal presence, loving-kindness, and, above all, His pardoning mercy and personal approval. Those who seek God with all their heart and soul will find Him.

3. The people must separate from sin by "turn[ing] from their wicked ways." Seeking God will be meaningless unless a nation repents of its sin, returns to God with a changed heart and mind, and puts away its wicked behavior.

Third, a nation that meets these requirements will find a three-fold *response* from God.

1. God will "hear from heaven," or take notice of the repentant prayer of people who humble themselves before Him.

2. God will heed the nation's plea for mercy by forgiving their sin.

3. God will "heal their land" by bringing about spiritual restoration, whereupon His people will experience peace and security. It has been said that pardoning mercy makes way for healing mercy.

Although this formula for spiritual restoration was given specifically to Israel, God will honor any nation that applies the principles to its situation. Nineveh is a case in point. The people were steeped in pagan superstition, groping in the hopeless darkness of idolatry. But at the preaching of Jonah, Nineveh believed God and repented of its sin—from the greatest to the least within the nation. This resulted in God's sparing them from destruction (Jon. 3:5-9). "And God saw their works, that they turned from their evil way; and God repented of the evil that he had said that he would do unto them, and he did it not" (Jon. 3:10).

Judah did not escape judgment because it did not heed the prophetic voice in its day. Without a spiritual renewal in this nation, America is destined to face swift decline, which will result in the country's demise. History has proven that nations (like Judah) who persist in *doing that which is right in their own eyes*, will likewise experience God's judgment.

How can we begin? First, start praying the Scriptures in this volume. Slowly and reflectively read through Habakkuk, Zephaniah, and Haggai, taking note of the places where God speaks of an attitude or an action that must be changed in Judah. Pause, and then put your name or nation in place of Judah. Start praying that God will bring personal or national forgiveness and true revival to you and to your country.

Second, as you reflect on what you have read and prayed, wait in silent meditation and listen to what attitude God wants you to change or what action He tells you to take. In so doing, your mind will not stray, and you will be acutely aware of the Lord's presence.

Third, act upon what God has given you, whether it be a sin to forsake, an attitude to change, or an action to perform.

Fourth, set out by faith, controlled by the Holy Spirit, and allow the Lord to use you like He did the prophets that you have just read. It may mean speaking out against evil in your situation, or getting involved with fellow Christians to stem the tide of wickedness in your area, or an entirely new thing that God will reveal to you at the proper time. Whatever you do may bring about mental or even physical suffering for the Lord. But God will provide the needed strength to face whatever He calls you to do. He did so for the prophets and the apostles before you.

Fifth, don't look to someone else to stem the tide of wickedness. God has chosen and uniquely gifted you for the task.

Winston Churchill said, "The one thing we have learned from history is that we don't learn from history." It is my prayer that you and the nation will prove Churchill wrong *and learn from the history of Judah.* Hopefully, God will stay His hand of judgment because of the commitment of faithful believers like you.

ENDNOTES

CHAPTER 1

[1] Herbert Wolf, *Haggai and Malachi: Rededication and Renewal* (Chicago: Moody Press, 1976), p. 13.

[2] *Ibid.*, p. 16.

[3] *Ibid.*, p. 17.

CHAPTER 2

[1] Thomas L. Constable, *The Bible Knowledge Commentary: 1 Kings* (Wheaton: Victor Books, 1985), pp. 499, 501.

[2] Charles Lee Feinberg, *Habakkuk, Zephaniah, Haggai and Malachi* (New York: American Board of Missions to the Jews, Inc., 1951), p. 89.

[3] Jerry Falwell, *Liberty Bible Commentary: Haggai* (New York: Thomas Nelson Publishers, 1983), p. 1788.

[4] Herbert Wolf, *Haggai and Malachi: Rededication and Renewal* (Chicago: Moody Press, 1976), p. 37.

Chapter 3

[1] Herbert Wolf, *Haggai and Malachi: Rededication and Renewal* (Chicago: Moody Press, 1976), p. 54.

[2] Ron Rhodes, *The Culting of America: The shocking implication for every concerned Christian* (Eugene: Harvest House Publishers, 1994), pp. 13-14, 217-18.

[3] Kerby Anderson, *The Decline of a Nation* (Dallas: Probe Ministries, 1991).

RECOMMENDED READING

Alden, Robert L. *The Expositor's Bible Commentary: Haggai.* Grand Rapids: Zondervan Publishing House, 1985.

Baldwin, Joyce G. *Haggai, Zechariah, Malachi: An Introduction and Commentary.* Downers Grove: InterVarsity Press, 1972.

Baxter, J. Sidlow. *Explore the Book: Haggai* (6 vols. in 1). Grand Rapids: Zondervan Publishing House, 1970.

Bullock, C Hassell. *An Introduction to the Old Testament Prophetic Books.* Chicago: Moody Press, 1986.

Feinberg, Charles L. *The Wycliffe Bible Commentary: Haggai* . Chicago: Moody Press, 1962.

Freeman, Hobart E. *An Introduction to the Old Testament Prophets.* Chicago: Moody Press, 1968.

_____. *Everyman's Bible Commentary: Nahum, Zephaniah, Habakkuk: Minor Prophets of the Seventh Century B.C.* Chicago: Moody Press, 1973.

Gaebelein, Frank E. *Four Minor Prophets: Obadiah, Jonah, Habakkuk, and Haggai.* Chicago: Moody Press, 1977.

Ironside, H. A. *Notes on the Minor Prophets.* Neptune, NJ: Loizeaux Brothers, 1909.

Keil, C. F. *Biblical Commentary on the Old Testament: Minor Prophets, Habakkuk,* vol. 2. Grand Rapids: Wm. B. Eerdmans, 1949.

Laetsch, Theo. *The Minor Prophets.* St. Louis: Concordia Publishing House, 1956.

Pusey, E. B. *The Minor Prophets: A Commentary,* vol. 2. Grand Rapids: Baker Book House, 1950.

Tatford, Frederick A. *The Minor Prophets: Prophet of the Watchtower: An Exposition of Habakkuk,* vol 2. Minneapolis: Klock and Klock Christian Publishers, Inc., 1982.

Unger, Merrill F. *Unger's Commentary on the Old Testament: Haggai*, vol 2. Chicago: Moody Press, 1981.

Wolf, Herbert. *Haggai and Malachi: Rededication and Renewal.* Chicago: Moody Press, 1976.

ABOUT THE AUTHOR

DAVID LEVY was born and reared in Dayton, Ohio. He received Jesus as his Messiah through the witness of a Hebrew Christian in November 1960. He is a graduate of Moody Bible Institute, the University of Illinois, and Trinity Evangelical Divinity School. David spent ten years pastoring in Illinois.

Since 1974, David and his faithful wife Beverly have been on the staff of the highly respected, New Jersey-based Friends of Israel Gospel Ministry. He serves as the Foreign Field Director, overseeing workers in nine countries. In addition to his administrative and personnel responsibilities, he is in demand throughout the world as a conference speaker. David travels extensively representing The Friends of Israel in Eastern and Western Europe, Israel, New Zealand, Australia, and North and South America.

David has been Associate Editor of The Friends of Israel's highly acclaimed bimonthly publication, *Israel my Glory*, since 1977. His expositional articles appear in each issue of the publication and in many other international magazines. He has authored a number of books, including *Joel: The Day of the Lord; Malachi: Messenger of Rebuke and Renewal; The Tabernacle: Shadows of the Messiah;* and *Guarding the Gospel of Grace.*